Freud and America

FREUD
AND AMERICA

BY

Hendrik M. Ruitenbeek

"As I stepped on to the platform at Worcester
to deliver my *Five Lectures upon Psychoanalysis* it seemed like the realization of some in-
credible day-dream: psychoanalysis was no
longer a product of delusion, it had become a
valuable part of reality."

SIGMUND FREUD
in *An Autobiographical Study*

The Macmillan Company, NEW YORK

Collier-Macmillan Limited, LONDON

16913

FOR

RICHARD MCCONCHIE

with whom I disagree

about Freud and psychoanalysis

Acknowledgments

This book springs from my deep conviction that Freud and psychoanalysis have firmer roots in the United States than anywhere else in the world today. I also wrote it as a token of admiration for a man who was the first psychoanalyst in the world.

This book could not have been written without the help and counsel of my dear friend Dr. Helene Zahler.

HENDRIK M. RUITENBEEK

Contents

Introduction
The American Unconscious

Introduction
The American Unconscious

PSYCHOANALYSIS, like its founder, has deep roots in the society of nineteenth-century Vienna. Yet in our time, psychoanalysis and its insights have become most accepted, their influence has been most general, not in Europe but in the United States. In Europe, psychoanalysis is still linked to psychiatry. The training of the European psychoanalyst is still carried on principally within the medical profession. A person who embarks on analytic treatment is usually seriously disturbed or even mentally ill; certainly he is so considered by his friends and family. Psychoanalysis is not table talk: most Europeans would consider it more polite to discuss their digestions at the dinner table than to talk about their neuroses. In Europe, psychoanalytic material is not absorbed as a matter of course by the student of society; the undergraduate does not routinely meet with ideas and interpretations derived from Freud. European teachers rarely employ insights derived from psychoanalysis in their daily work; few educational authorities there would talk about a "therapeutic classroom." Deliberate application of psychoanalytic ideas is equally uncommon in courts, the church, or in social agencies.

In contrast, psychoanalysis—Freudian, neo-Freudian, and post-Freudian—is woven into all aspects of American life. Teachers, novelists, poets, social workers, ministers, advertising men, sociologists, biographers—all draw upon psychoanalytic ideas, however misinterpreted, and even use vocabularies deeply colored by Freudian phrases. That Freud's influence should be so much more evident in America than in Europe is the more ironic when one recalls the low esteem in which Freud himself held the United States.[1]

Ironic too is the welcome which a technologically oriented and open society has given to an interpretation of human nature and its problems which was developed in a highly stratified society where industrialization had advanced in only limited areas. Neither the content nor the tone of Freudian psychoanalysis would seem congenial to Americans. They are optimists who believe in happy endings, ultimate solutions, and the goodness, or the malleability, of man. Freud was not notably optimistic, and he had no high opinion of human nature; he is uncompromisingly realistic, and as his ideas developed, he concluded that in the struggle between the forces of love and death in the human being death had a strong sting indeed and the grave a good chance of victory.

Actually, as we shall see, the acceptance of psychoanalysis in the United States is owed in great degree to subsequent modifications of his theories and techniques—and indeed of his basically tragic outlook. Still, the post- and neo-Freudians retain much of Freud's original body of insight. Essentially, psychoanalysis has become acceptable in the United States because it met and continues to meet Americans' psychological needs. Those needs are related to the kind of society which has developed in America, to the variety of personality that society has tended to foster, and to the problems with which that society confronts the people who live in it.

American society derived its essential ideas and attitudes from Western Europe, of course, but it developed those in ways which produced a unique result. The society is open and, in certain areas, flexible. It is the more easily penetrated by some kinds of new ideas because, for all its habit of complacent self-congratulation, it lacks confidence: a colonial past marks the attitudes of an important part of its traditional

[1] Freud's attitude toward America is discussed further in Chapter 1. See especially pp. 29–30.

upper class; an awareness of comparatively lowly origins colors the responses of many of its newly prosperous and educated persons, particularly among intellectuals. Such lack of confidence tends to encourage self-examination; like the young man uncertain of the set of his tie, the American looks at himself (sometimes in the mirror of the foreign observer), eager to find reason to praise, but not altogether unwilling to find fault. This readiness to look at society and themselves helped make some Americans receptive to psychoanalysis as a challenging, novel frame of reference, one that offered a "scientific" warrant for a new approach to personal relationships.

American society is open, that is, it has imposed relatively few barriers to the upward movement of able and energetic persons; it has encouraged individual competitiveness and made rising in the world a social obligation. A society of this sort is strenuous: it demands much of the individual and on the whole offers him little external psychological support. It generates tensions that it does little to ease. It operates to weaken the authority of traditional institutions like the family and the church, yet by its emotional attachment to the free market economy, it continues to be hostile to the growth of a paternalistic state which might substitute its own psychologically supportive authority for those which have been weakened.

In an open and mobile society, psychoanalysis can more easily attain to broad intellectual influence and to general social acceptance than is possible in more stable societies which make upward mobility less of a social duty, which tend to maintain the effectiveness of traditional sources of authority, and which show less readiness to examine themselves or to seek new guidelines for the individual.

Areas of Intellectual Penetration

In the United States, Freudian theory has affected literature, education, religion, and academic scholarship throughout the range of the social disciplines. Its echoes are heard in the press, in the prisons, in the courts. Even the practice of medicine has been affected: pediatricians tell mothers that feeding a child means more than providing it with a proper assemblage of nutrients; "psychosomatic" complaints are less frequently regarded as malingering; and the physical afflictions of old age are recognized as being complicated by fear of death and resentment at years gone by without satisfaction. The effect of psychoanalytic insight is evident in the work of many of the sociologists who will be cited; indeed psychoanalytic thought permeates most of the interpretations presented here, including my own. Anthropologists describe primitive societies in terms of character types developed in consequence of certain methods of child rearing. Economists study their model of man in awareness that he is governed by irrational motivations. The custodians of morality are troubled about ethical sanctions. Psychoanalysis has forced re-examination of old standards and thus brought some people at least to the conviction that new standards are called for. When those standards finally do appear, they will have been shaped, at least in part, by Freud's influence.

Freud, as we shall see, was surprised to learn that a few Americans were interested in psychoanalysis. He might well have been astounded to learn that a psychotherapy in which his work was formative was to become a social as well as a medical need in some American circles. The individual, as we have said, experiences a high degree of pressure in contemporary society. Yet most Americans are convinced that the social game is worth its candle, that the rewards they can hope for are reasonable payment for the demands made on them. They tolerate the strictures of their lives fairly well, yet often they find it necessary to look for help. Increasingly the more prosperous and better educated, particularly in urban centers, seek psychological counseling and psychotherapy for themselves and their children. In some social groups, one turns to the psychotherapist in times of emotional distress as routinely as one takes an aching tooth to the dentist.

Further, psychoanalysis is no longer a treatment which only the severely troubled seek out; it is often considered part of one's education, something which may be expected to increase one's potential for growth.

So many people seek access to this path toward personal development that the demand for psychotherapists has far outstripped the supply. Certified psychologists with psychoanalytic training are working as lay analysts, as might be expected. Social workers and educators have joined the ranks. Numerous social scientists have adapted the psychoanalytic orientation of their thinking to the needs of therapy, and a number of sociologists are practicing as analysts. The effect of such practice on psychoanalytic techniques and theories may produce interesting results in a few years (provided that the demands of patients for treatment do not absorb all the therapist's energies).

If the felt need for therapy has become so great as to constitute an element of what John Seeley calls "the American Unconscious,"[2] part of that need is derived from problems rooted in sexuality and family relationships. The American scene has been colored by repressive attitudes toward sexuality and by a social situation which tended to foster an anal concentration on getting money and spending it (keeping has been less generally a focus of concern because enterprising men were less fearful of loss than desirous of gain, less eager to preserve estates for their children than to display their own prowess in the market place). The United States is a nation where the Protestant ethic of thrift and industry has prevailed, conquering most immigrant groups. American social mobility furthered the centering of attention on making money.

Where moneymaking becomes "the whole duty of man," as it so often did during the nineteenth century, other aspects of life take second place. The Christian tradition, particularly in its Puritan version, regarded sexuality with fear and dis-

[2] Hendrik M. Ruitenbeek, ed., *Psychoanalysis and Social Science* (New York: E. P. Dutton & Company, 1962), pp. 186ff.

trust, and this anxiety-generating set of emotions was heightened by the importance given to moneymaking: indulgence of sexuality was a distraction from duty. Hence prudishness became acute in nineteenth-century America. The virtuous woman held a noteworthy position in society—and all women were presumed to be virtuous, that is sexually indifferent, or at least inactive.

By the end of the century, however, psychic conflict generated by the sexual repressiveness of the society became evident. Such conflict, expressed physically in nervous dyspepsia (which had long been an American complaint) and artistically in novelists' claiming a new right to freedom of expression, came into view along with conflicts more evidently social: farmers' resentment of the political power of urban wealth, workers' efforts to win a greater share of the product of the economy, reformers' criticism of the exploitive character of nineteenth-century industrial life and its destructive effect upon the free individual.

Ferment and Freudian Thought

All the discontents just mentioned made for a sense of ferment in the years between 1895 and 1909 when psychoanalysis first became known in the United States. Freudian thought, with its emphasis on the significance of sexual development in generating neurosis, moved onto the American intellectual scene just as many Americans were becoming rebellious against prevailing sexual mores. The "new woman," self-supporting and demanding consideration as an independent person rather than an adjunct to a family—sister, wife, mother, or maiden aunt—antedates psychoanalysis. The sexual orientation of "the new woman" tended to be negative, to be sure (she expressed her resentment against the demand that the nice, middle-class woman remain virgin—until a wedding ring gave her the right to be otherwise—by insisting that the nice middle-class man give what he expected to get—that he, too, keep himself "pure"), but because of her, psychoanalysis may well have won an easier hearing. Such restrictive forms of sexual morality have gone by the board in contemporary society. The *Reader's Digest* has published few if any articles in praise of premarital chastity since the former champion boxer Gene Tunney's wartime essay.[3] Once sex and the sexual side of life were considered indecent. Nowadays sexual prowess is considered not only a virtue but almost an obligation. In order to be considered successful or even acceptable the adolescent must engage in the elaborate ritual of dating, a ritual which may, because of its competitive character and its effort to avoid emotional involvement, contribute to the American adult's ambivalent and unstable attitudes toward sex. Everywhere one sees sexual symbols, frequently used as a means of selling commodities like cars, which apparently serve no direct sexual purpose. One also sees a high degree of sexual acting out. The Kinsey reports showed that Americans were sexually active not only in all the conventional ways, but in deviant fashions as well. (The great number of these expensive and soberly statistical books which have been sold seems to show that Americans will accept almost anything as pornography if they are told it is about sex.)[4] Sexual repression, so evident in some of Freud's patients, has lessened in contemporary America, but one may question whether compulsive sexual activity is fundamentally more healthy than compulsory sexual repression. Freud's theories may have contributed to liberalizing the sexual mores in America, but his influence was probably only a contributing factor. His authority may have given permission, as it were, but the American superego must have changed before that permission could be accepted.

It is difficult to discover just how changing social forces

[3] Gene Tunney, "The Bright Shield of Continence," *Readers' Digest*, 41 (August, 1942), pp. 43–46.

[4] Alfred Kinsey, *et al*, *Sexual Behavior in the Human Male* (Philadelphia: W. B. Saunders, 1948). Subsequent volumes in the series of studies by Kinsey and his colleagues have attracted fewer readers.

affect the individual superego as that integrates the commands of society into the personality. Yet one cannot but help believe that change and speed of change in those forces do affect the superego, do in considerable degree determine how parents deal with their children, how schools educate them, and how, as a result, individual characters are formed. We have mentioned the social ferment at work in American society at the turn of the century. That ferment continued working variously during the 1920's and 1930's. By the time World War II ended, old sanctions had lost effectiveness; old sanctities seemed less hallowed. The old-fashioned virtues of thrift and prudence, enjoyment postponed and self-denial glorified, no longer contributed to the welfare of an economy which could support its productive capacities on a free market basis only if people were willing to buy, to anticipate their income, to go into debt, to make enjoyment a goal in life.

Sociologists and historians will undoubtedly have more and more to tell us about the relationship between sexual repression and the emphasis on money-getting in America. They have already told us much about the role of the American woman in making sexuality so ambiguous a constituent of the American unconscious. For generations, the American family has been mother-oriented, mother-controlled, mother-directed. Whether prosperous or poor, the American father has usually been too busy to play an intimate role in the rearing of his children. Even if the mother did treat her husband as ultimate punishing authority, she took major responsibility for disciplining her children. Mother taught manners; mother was custodian of morals; mother proffered food and gave love— or withheld it. But above all, mother was there. If the American woman is afflicted by penis envy, as, according to Freud all women are doomed to be, the structure of American society has given her a good opportunity for revenge, at least on the unconscious level.

Mother's constant effective presence has had widespread psychological consequences. The patterns of American family life gave her freedom to be possessive. And it is when mothers are possessive that children have greatest difficulty in working through the oedipal phase of their development. Indeed, contemporary psychoanalytic emphasis on the role of the possessive mother in the oedipal conflict may well reflect the interplay between theory and social situation in the growth of Freudian theory in America. To Freud, the boy was aggressive; only in his fantasy was the mother seductive. Jocasta plays a passive role in Sophocles; she is but an unwitting sinner. Anouilh has Jocasta encourage the young stranger to ignore her age and remember what she can offer him. But when an American playwright like Albee uses the myth, Jocasta keeps the scepter: the young stranger does not gain the kingdom, he spends his manhood for a job.

The psychotherapist continually encounters the patient who describes a strong possessive mother, a father weak at home, however competent at the office, and the patient himself beset by the difficulties experienced in his relationship to them both. Homosexuality, impotence, and an increasing feeling on the part of the American male that he is being emasculated by a castrating mother, or a wife reared in her image, are only a few consequences of the American family constellation. Many post- and neo-Freudian thinkers dismiss penis envy and regard the Oedipus complex as irrelevant to the problems of their patients. Clinical experience confirms me in the contrary view. The oedipal situation has during the past decade become a more significant factor than ever in shaping the American unconscious.

Psychoanalysis in an Open Society

We have been dealing here with some of the relations between receptiveness to Freudian theory and the existence in the United States of a highly structured, yet open and unremittingly demanding society. Technological change speeds on at an accelerated pace, offering no halting places and depleting the authority of the established institutions of psychological comfort. Many Americans, particularly the well educated and upward mobile are likely to experience the demands of this society at their most exacting; these people are sufficiently aware of their situation to know something of what is happening to them, and they can meet the costs of the help they seek.

Traditional philosophy has not had too much to offer these people who so often constitute the "intellectual growing edge" of the society. Traditional religion has tended to lose authority among them. Many have rejected Protestant orthodoxy (neo-orthodoxy has often made its peace with Freud). Until recently, Roman Catholicism has been the faith of a segment of the lower class which has not yet made intensive use of education as its ladder of social ascent. The Catholic third of the American population exerts considerable, even disproportionate influence on many aspects of contemporary life, to be sure, but it has not yet had sufficient intellectual influence to color the whole society with its traditionalism.

Because American society is thus open and demanding, psychoanalysis has had a wider field of operation in the United States than in Europe. It has faced fewer obstacles and it has met more evident needs. Psychoanalytic insights have appeared particularly relevant to individuals who stand so largely alone and undefended against the pressures of their society. The sense of self has been lost by many people. The search for identity affects and torments them. Parents, themselves unsure, seek counsel on how to rear their children. Children seem peculiarly important to these parents; bringing children up "properly" often means that the uncertain parent is making up to himself for what his parents did not give him. Formal education, too, seems highly significant to such parents, for they hope that education will give life the shape which tradition supplies in other, more slowly moving cultures. In the home, the mother rules openly to a degree not general in other Western societies. Women staff schools too and there establish standards of behavior. These standards—docility, receptivity, dependence on affection and the goodwill of others —run counter to the requirements for success in a competitive economy and also are in conflict with the image of the male as aggressive and independent. As a result, many boys seem hampered in the process of learning to be men; nor do girls have a much easier time learning to be women.

Conflict and stress create pain for the individual, and he seeks help. In the United States, far more than in Europe, people are willing to think of themselves as neurotic and to accept neurosis in others. Yet they have what often seems like a desperate desire to be normal, especially when the term is applied to social practice or sexual behavior. Awareness of discomfort and the search for ease have led to the desire to understand oneself (or one's lack of self) and one's society. Consequently, we see not only the development of the be-havioral sciences and the recourse to psychotherapy and psy-chiatric social work to a higher degree than in contemporary Europe, but also a high level of awareness, sometimes evident in the absurdities of the public "search for national purpose," sometimes evident in receptivity to new philosophic orienta-tions. Contemporary Americans have shown interest in Kierke-gaard, Sartre, Nietzsche, and Buber, as well as Freud. But it is psychoanalysis—as presented by Freud and his successors —which has contributed most to making the unconscious con-scious for many an American in search of himself. This aware-ness has often made people self-conscious and more than ever unsure about their place in the world. But it has also stimu-lated some men and women to accept a self-questioning atti-tude which may operate as a useful corrective to the pressures for conformity and acquiescence which often tend to smother individuality. Whereas western Europeans are, in general, little inclined to investigate and interpret themselves or their socie-ties from psychoanalytic points of view, Americans are ready to employ Freudian theory to help them in their long-existing desire to learn more about themselves and each other. A vast literature in the social sciences has grown up as a result, and

American behavioral scientists have moved into the forefront in the application of Freudian and post-Freudian concepts in this field.

In the swift movement of an open society which makes no effective effort to control the pace of technological change, psychoanalysis has taken on unexpected functions; it has moved in ways which Freud would not have anticipated. In the structure of the American unconscious, psychoanalysis has, for some people, replaced earlier ideologies and even certain religious consolations. Consequently, psychoanalysis has undergone marked changes. Yet, as we shall see, even these modifications are best understood in the light of Freud's own discoveries and formulations.

1 · Freud at Worcester

1 · Freud at Worcester

FREUD at Worcester. It sounds like the beginning of a novel. The novel does not exist, of course, but in 1909 receiving an invitation to lecture on psychoanalysis at an American university may well have seemed like fiction to Freud. As he wrote to his Swiss friend, the minister Oskar Pfister:

It is one of the pleasant phantasies to imagine that somewhere far off, without one's having a glimmering of it, there are decent people finding their way into our thoughts and efforts, who after all suddenly make their appearance. That is what happened to me with Stanley Hall. Who could have known that over there in America only an hour away from Boston, there was a respectable old gentleman waiting impatiently for the next number of the *Jahrbuch*, reading and understanding it all, and who would then, as he expressed it himself, "ring the bells for us."[1]

The university was a small one, to be sure, and Worcester, Massachusetts, was no hallowed seat of learning. Clark had been named for its founder, millionaire Jonas Gilman Clark

---

[1] Ernest Jones, *The Life and Work of Sigmund Freud*, vol. 2 (New York: Basic Books, Inc., 1957), p. 58. *Jahrbuch für psychoanalytische und psychopathologische Forschungen*, 1908–14. Oskar Pfister (1873–1956) was a Protestant clergyman, the first pastor to use psychoanalytic techniques to help troubled parishioners, and one of the first lay analysts to practice before World War I. In spite of essential differences about religion, Pfister maintained a close relationship with Freud and continued among the faithful after Jung broke relations with Freud. Pfister's correspondence with Freud was published in *Psychoanalysis and Faith* (New York: Basic Books, 1963).

who gave most of the money which had financed its establishment twenty-odd years earlier. And indeed the Worcester that Freud encountered in the fall of 1909 was a grimy, rather crowded industrial town where a few old buildings and the library of the American Antiquarian Society were all that remained to remind people that once Worcester had been a nest of rebels, the place where, shortly after the end of the American Revolution, Daniel Shays tried and failed to rally embattled debtors for an attack on what they considered unjust and discriminatory taxes. G. Stanley Hall, president of Clark, could hardly have had Shays in mind when he issued his invitation to Freud, yet Hall was helping bring to the United States thinking which would lead to far greater changes than the debt moratorium which Captain Shays had wanted the Massachusetts legislature to adopt. But Hall was a psychologist, not an historian, and he was more interested in current developments within his own discipline than with the effect which future changes in that discipline might have upon American life. Hall's own work had been a pioneering study of youth, *Adolescence*.[2] The title alone leads one to see why Hall should have been interested in Freud, and the book itself shows some of that concern with change which ultimately helped make Americans so receptive to psychoanalysis and so much more ready than Europeans to bring its insights to bear in fields outside psychiatry.

Invitation to Columbus

Although Clark University was no world-renowned institution (it did become an important center for geographic studies later on), its invitation was the first serious academic recognition psychoanalysis had received. As Freud said, accepting the honorary degree Clark gave him (and it was the only such

[2] G. Stanley Hall, *Adolescence: Its Psychology and Its Relation to Physiology, Anthropology, Sociology, Sex, Crime, Religion and Education* (New York: D. Appleton & Company, 1904).

degree he ever got): *"Dies is die erste offizielle Anerkennung unsere Bemuhungen."* [This is the first official recognition of our endeavors.]

When Freud sailed, on August 21, 1909, for the United States with Ferenczi and Jung (Jung was at that time still close to him and the psychoanalytic movement), he was surprised and perhaps pleased to find his cabin steward reading *The Psychopathology of Everyday Life*. We have an amusing picture of the three analysts interpreting each other's dreams at the shipboard breakfast table—one of the first instances of group therapy, perhaps.[3] The landing of the three passed unnoticed in the United States, except by one newspaper which told New York that "Professor Freund [sic] of Vienna" had arrived.

In New York on August 30, shortly before Freud and Jung left for Worcester, A. A. Brill, who had known Freud in Vienna and Jung at Bürghölzli, introduced them to Dr. Adolf Meyer, who had made a notable reputation as a classifier of mental diseases and as a hospital administrator. Meyer was accompanied by Trigant Burrow, one of his co-workers at the New York State Mental Hospital on Ward's Island, who was to be one of the pioneers of psychoanalysis in America. That evening, Brill took his guests to the roof garden atop Oscar Hammerstein's theater.[4]

Freud's letters give little evidence of his impressions of that evening. Perhaps his displeasure with the United States extended even to social meetings with his colleagues—for American food disturbed Freud's digestion and displeased his Viennese palate; the magnificent distances between reception rooms and hotel toilets put a strain on his middle-aged bladder.[5] Yet even if the United States was a good place for a civilized man to stay away from, Freud was gratified by recognition

---

[3] Jones, *op. cit.*, pp. 55, 56. Throughout this chapter, I have drawn upon the second volume of Jones's biography of Freud.

[4] Jones, who was present at the dinner, tells how they went to a movie afterward, the first film that Freud had ever seen.

[5] Jones, *op. cit.*, p. 60.

from a widely acknowledged psychiatric authority like Meyer; Freud thought of the Clark lectures as an important step toward winning more general understanding and acceptance of psychoanalysis. His work had secured discouragingly little favorable attention in Europe, where psychoanalysis was ignored, jeered at, or denounced as sheer dabbling in obscenity.

Professor Freud Explains

The people who attended the Clark University anniversary convocation were apparently somewhat less hidebound. Fairly large audiences listened to Freud lecture in German, and those who heard all five of the talks became acquainted with Freud's basic concepts and with the fundamentals of psychoanalytic technique: free association, the interpretation of dreams, and the evaluation of what are often considered chance acts and errors, slips of the tongue, forgetting, and the like. Freud's hearers learned of psychic conflict, of the repression of unacceptable wishes, the survival of such wishes in the unconscious and their conversion into hysterical symptoms.

Most of the unacceptable impulses were sexual in character, Freud told them; sexual disturbances were of prime significance in creating repression and the symptoms which broke through that repression. Furthermore, those unacceptable sexual wishes originated in childhood. For the child was a sexual being, although his sexuality was not yet connected with reproduction. Only gradually during the course of the child's maturing was sexuality "taken over into the service of procreation." Development did not always proceed smoothly to its completion. A person might, therefore, regress into some childish, "perverted" expression of sexuality. Or as a result of situational strains, his successfully surmounted childish desires might erupt and express themselves in neurosis. The child is a helpless being as well as a sexual one; hence, he becomes attached to those who care for him, particularly to his parents, whom he takes as "the object of his erotic wishes." The boy desires his mother; the girl, her father. Each considers the parent of the same sex as a rival; rivals, too, are all the child's siblings, and especially the baby who follows him. The child wants his rivals hurt or killed. This psychological constellation constituted the *nuclear complex* (a term Freud attributed to Carl Jung), and Freud cited the Oedipus legend as an ancient presentation of the infantile wish. And that nuclear complex was involved in all neurotic behavior.

In his concluding lecture, Freud described neurosis as a flight from reality; the patient resists "cure" in analytic treatment because he is not certain that he can find in reality anything better than the warped satisfaction to be gained from his symptoms. Most civilized men, Freud said to his audience, find reality "quite unsatisfactory." Energetic, competent people may be able to shape reality somewhat to their liking. People gifted with "that artistic talent which is still a riddle" can transform fantasy into art and so return to reality. Many who are neither talented nor sufficiently strong take refuge in neurosis, especially when they encounter special difficulties. But those who seek such shelter are not qualitatively different from the healthy. All men struggle with unacceptable impulses; it depends on "the relation of the forces wrestling with each other whether the struggle leads to health, to neurosis, or to compensatory overfunctioning."

Concluding his lectures, Freud defended psychoanalysis against the charge that it was socially dangerous to call repressed material into consciousness. He concluded that, on the contrary, only when repellent infantile sexual wishes were brought out of the unconscious could they be effectively dealt with, finally outgrown, and subdued. The psychological energy which animated those desires might be sublimated, diverted toward a non-sexual goal. Or sexuality might be granted greater recognition:

The claims of our civilization make life too hard for the greater part of humanity, and so further the aversion to reality and the origin of neuroses without producing an excess of cultural gain by this excess of sexual repression. We ought not to go so far as fully to neglect the original animal part of our nature; we ought not to forget that the happiness of individuals cannot be dispensed with as one of the aims of our culture. The plasticity of the sexual components, manifest in their capacity for sublimation, may cause a great temptation to accomplish great cultural effects by a more and more far-reaching sublimation. But just as little as with our machines we expect to change more than a certain fraction of the applied heat into useful mechanical work, just as little ought we to strive to separate the sexual impulse in its whole extent of energy from its peculiar goal. This cannot succeed, and if the narrowing of sexuality is pushed too far, it will have all the evil effects of a robbery.[6]

Initial Impacts

Revolutionary as these concepts were, the character of their reception rather surprised Freud. He was used, as we have said, to being ignored or attacked. In the United States, he found himself "accepted by the best men as an equal."[7] These "best men" included not only Adolf Meyer and Stanley Hall but also Edward Titchener, a leader in the field of psychological testing and experimentation; James J. Putnam, the Harvard neurologist; and William James.

James's attitude was rather ambivalent, however. He told Ernest Jones ". . . the future of psychology belongs to your work," but in a letter to Theodore Flournoy, the Swiss psychologist, James was less friendly to the new psychotherapy:

Speaking of "functional" psychology [he wrote] Clark University had a little international congress the other day in honor of the twentieth year of its existence. I went there for one day in order to see what Freud was like. I hope that Freud and his pupils will push

---

[6] Freud's Worcester lectures are reprinted in Hendrik M. Ruitenbeek, ed., *Varieties of Personality Theory* (New York: E. P. Dutton & Company, 1964), pp. 42–43.

[7] Sigmund Freud, *Selbstdarstellung* (Leipzig: Felix Meiner, 1925).

their ideas to their utmost limits, so that we may learn what they are. They can't fail to throw light on human nature; but I confess that he made on me personally the impression of a man obsessed with fixed ideas. I can make nothing in my own case with his dream theories; and obviously "symbolism" is a most dangerous method. A newspaper report of the congress said that Freud had condemned the American religious therapy (which has such extensive results) as very "dangerous" because so "unscientific." Bah![8]

Putnam, too, was somewhat ambivalent although he was one of the first American psychiatrists to accept psychoanalysis and Freud, and probably the first physician to use Freud's concepts in treating patients.

When Ernest Jones met Putnam in Boston at the home of another important student of clinical psychology, Morton Prince, he was struck by the Harvard professor's openminded attitude toward what many younger men (Putnam was past sixty) regarded as a shocking novelty. Putnam joined Freud and his friends at Clark, was an attentive member of Freud's audience, and entertained him at his own summer home in the Adirondacks after the lecture series.[9] (Again one wonders what Freud thought of the American's delight in "roughing it" in the woods.)

Freud's American visit did much to stimulate discussion of psychoanalysis among American psychologists and psychiatrists, and that discussion increased understanding of the new approach to emotional disturbance. Under the leadership of people like A. A. Brill, the New York Psychoanalytic Society was organized in 1911. Members met for discussion of problems encountered in practice and for the discussion of papers on psychoanalytic theory. Later, some of them went

[8] The religious therapy to which James refers may be Christian Science, the more fashionable Emersonian New Thought, or the Emanuel movement, which was having considerable success in dealing with what was then called *neurasthenia* and what we now usually call *depressive states*.

[9] Jones, *op. cit.* p. 109.

to Vienna for training analyses with Freud himself; during the 1920's, a number of American analysts worked with Otto Rank.[10] In this way, the question *quis custodiet custodies* received its answer: men who presented themselves as capable of helping patients cope with their emotional problems had tried and, hopefully, succeeded in recognizing and handling at least some of their own.

The lucid, forthright exposition of his ideas which Freud offered in the Worcester lectures stimulated hostile criticism as well as serious study of psychoanalysis. His concern with, and his broad interpretation of, sexuality gave occasion for much of this hostility. The United States had a Puritan heritage, and puritanism was hostile to sex. In the United States (and the England) of 1909, morality was operationally defined as conduct which came within the bounds of what was considered to be acceptable *sexual* behavior and emotion. Freud considered the prevailing American definition of sexual morality "contemptible"; he stood for ". . . an incomparably freer sexual life, although I myself have made very little use of such freedom. . . ."[11] (The twentieth-century reader may be irreverently Freudian enough to detect a certain defensiveness beneath the final qualification.) Earlier, Putnam had expressed some misgivings about the emphasis which psychoanalytic theory placed on sexuality (though in his public discussion of psychoanalysis, he denied that the emphasis was excessive). In a letter to Jones, who had reported some of Putnam's uncertainties, Freud wrote:

Putnam's letter was very amusing. Yet I fear if he keeps away from Jung on account of his mysticism and denial of incest, he will shrink back from us (on the other side) for our defending sexual liberty. His second-thought, pencil-written question is very suggestive about that. I wonder what you will answer to it. I hope no

[10] Martin Wang, ed., *Fruition of an Idea: Fifty Years of Psychoanalysis in New York* (New York: International University Press, 1962), p. 41.
[11] Jones, *op. cit.*, pp. 417–18.

denial that our sympathies side with individual freedom and that we find no improvement in the strictness of American chastity.[12]

If Putnam, open as he was to the merits of psychoanalysis, could be thus dubious about it at times, the unmixed hostility of other psychiatrists and psychologists is scarcely to be wondered at. Nor is it surprising to learn that their hostility was directed against Freud's making sexuality the central factor in neurosis. In 1909, for instance, at a meeting of the American Psychological Association, Boris Sidis, a well-known scholar in the field, talked about the "mad epidemic of Freudism now invading America" and denounced Freud as akin to "those pious sexualists," the Mormons. The following year, Putnam was accused of telling the American Neurological Society "pornographic stories about pure virgins" in the guise of a scientific paper concerning one of his cases.[13] Even Stanley Hall found Freud's stress on sexuality too much (as did Jung and Adler, it will be remembered) and diverged from psychoanalytic orthodoxy in 1914 to accept Adler as his master.[14]

If psychiatrists themselves were thus gingerly or openly hostile, we can scarcely wonder at reports that the Boston police went so far as to threaten Morton Prince with prosecution for publishing obscenities in the *Journal of Abnormal Psychology* when he opened its pages to psychoanalytic papers. Prince was a distinguished psychologist who had done noteworthy work in investigating and reporting cases of dissociated personality. The *Journal* was a pioneer forum in which

[12] Jones, *Ibid.,* p. 103.

[13] His accuser was Dr. Joseph Collins, who was notorious, according to Jones, for relishing and repeating improper stories (*Ibid.,* p. 115). Ironically, Collins later published *The Doctor Looks at Love and Life,* a book whose large sale was certainly not unconnected with popular interest in what was thought to be psychoanalysis.

[14] Hall continued to accept Freud's contention that childhood experiences could become unconscious, survive, and have a subsequent effect "far greater than our current psychology has ever suspected." See G. Stanley Hall, *Recreations of a Psychologist* (New York: D. Appleton & Co., 1920).

American students of emotional disturbance could share their discoveries. That such a serious professional publication could become a target for even a Boston police force may well have seemed absurd to Freud. Even more absurd was the reason Prince was not brought into court: as a former mayor of the city, he was apparently too respectable, or too important, to be arrested on such a charge. The incident does not seem to have changed Prince's editorial policy, and the Boston police found more popular material to prosecute.

Message to Restive America

Basic to the history of psychoanalysis in the United States is its encounter with Puritanism. The Puritan heritage, as has been said, includes a hatred of sexuality and a sense of sin. Psychoanalysis, in Freud's formulation, regards sexuality as the source of human energy, the ground from which all creativity sprang. Consequently, the sense of sin associated with sexuality is merely a neurotic lingering of the child's misunderstanding and distortion of his experience.

Psychoanalysis and Puritanism thus stand in basic conflict. One might well expect, indeed, that the United States would be the last country in which Freudian theory could become influential. Certainly its attitudes in respect to some aspects of sexual behavior seemed narrowminded to many Europeans. In 1909, when Freud came to lecture at Worcester, American novelists were far less free to describe the fullness of life in the special vocabularies of all the kinds of people who live it than were the novelists of France, for example. Americans who asserted a greater measure of freedom than was customary found their work either unnoticed—Stephen Crane's novella, *Maggie: A Girl of the Streets*, for instance—or in conflict with that most effective variety of censorship, the disapproval of a publisher's female relatives. Here one may cite the experience of Theodore Dreiser whose *Sister Carrie*, though printed, was kept off the market for a decade after a publisher had contracted to bring it out, because, it is said, the publisher's wife thought the book was immoral. Its heroine is portrayed as a good person, though she had been kept by two men, and it was not she but one of her lovers who ended wretchedly.

But for all its prudery, and despite powerful Puritan survivals, America was in a state of restiveness in the years before World War I. Freud brought psychoanalysis to a country entering upon the phase of economic and social transition which was to culminate in the organizational society of the middle twentieth century. Moreover, one should note that the Puritan view of human nature and the Puritan attitude toward conduct have some points in common with the picture of man developed in psychoanalytic theory. Freud explored the primitive urges of the unconscious and, particularly, the unbridled character of man's instinctual energy. Puritanism recognized and greatly feared that force in man which makes him difficult to govern whether the governor be another or himself. Sexuality was only one aspect of that force, to be sure, but its unruly aspect gave it a certain symbolic character; to the Puritan, the "lust of the flesh" and the "pride of life" meant something beyond offenses against law, human and divine: they were evidence of the fallen nature of man.

Further, the Puritan tradition exacted unremitting self-scrutiny from anyone who meant really to practice his religion. Whether we look at Freud as a psychological theorist or as a psychotherapist, self-examination is the core of his method. Sigmund Freud's first analysand was himself; from rigorous self-examination, he found out about other people, a truly Puritan procedure. Puritanism saw man as neither good nor simple. Freudian theory explored man's complexities and found what may be termed evil hiding behind many masks of good.

Awareness of such common attitudes, incidentally, helps one to understand how so many American clergymen have been able to transport psychoanalysis into their own frame of reference. That his theories, which sought to help men know themselves so that they might become free from irrational guilt, should become a support for those whose professional commitment is to maintain a sense of sin may well have appealed to a thinker who is reputed to have had some sense of humor. (Freud among the clergy is discussed in detail in Chapter 6.) Here we need note only that Puritanism, with its emphasis on an essential wickedness requiring rigid control, is not too alien from a psychological theory which sees man as perpetually tempted to evade the demands of reality. The spirit animating Puritan concepts of man was very different from the spirit animating psychoanalysis, yet their spokesmen could understand each other.

Such understanding is a significant factor in helping us see why the Puritan heritage not only did not prevent Freudian theory from winning support and exerting influence in the United States but may finally have helped in the contemporary assimilation of psychoanalysis.

Freud lecturing on psychoanalysis at Clark University in Worcester, Massachusetts, is a forecast of things to come; his lectures constitute more than the beginning of a new American profession, the introduction and growth of a more scientific kind of psychotherapy. When Freud's work began to be known, Americans had begun to feel the old restrictive social conventions as a burden. Indeed, for all its prudishness, American society had long been characterized by certain permissive elements in its sexual mores. Young people were free to choose their spouses. Customs like the obligatory dowry had been dropped. Young men and women associated far more freely in the United States than in Europe. On the whole, American young people might go alone to dances or to the theater; they might even drive off in buggies unsupervised. Coeducation had become quite common in American secondary schools and at the publicly supported state universities which women were allowed to attend. American customs assumed, of course, that such free association of young people at the period of highest sexual excitability would not carry them so far beyond convention that middle-class girls could no longer be assumed to be virgins at marriage.

As for marriage, the Puritans had, since the seventeenth century, considered it a purely civil contract; and although contracts were indeed sacred, they were not sacraments; marriages, like contracts, could be terminated. In a number of American states, divorce had long been relatively easy to obtain, whereas civil divorce was forbidden in some Catholic countries of Europe and was often a difficult and costly procedure elsewhere.

What really differentiated American from European attitudes toward sexual behavior and the relationship between men and women was the publicly acknowledged social influence exerted by the middle-class woman. She was the custodian of the nation's morals, its manners, and its esthetic culture. She taught its young. Her tastes and timidities in effect dictated which elements in the more learned and sophisticated sectors of intellectual life would be allowed to seep down into common knowledge. Hence her demand for "a single standard of morals" (meaning sexual behavior) signaled a major social change. At first the "new woman" demanded that the middle-class man accept for himself the same postponement of sexual gratification that he exacted from his bride. Later, the new woman began to assert her own right to experiment with sex before marriage without risking a loss of social standing. What the advanced had boldly claimed in the decade before the first World War and in the years afterward, more conventional people accepted as proper by the 1940's and 1950's. The middle-class woman (like the post-Freudian child) was no longer presumed to be a non-sexual creature. She might even demand sexual satisfaction in marriage. Because the middle-class woman does exert so far-ranging an influence in America, what changes her changes the *mores*. White-collar and blue-collar wives continue to see their sexual roles differently, but one may risk the guess that in this sphere, too, middle-class standards of sexual behavior will filter down, along with other middle-class tastes.

The Worcester lectures aroused no widespread popular

attention. They were published in the *American Journal of Psychology* in 1910.[15] With those lectures and Brill's translations of the *Three Contributions to the Theory of Sex* (1910) and the *Interpretation of Dreams* (1913), Americans could acquire first-hand knowledge of Freud's theories of psychosexual development. At first, only a few physicians and psychologists were interested. More were irritated and shocked: Freud asserted that patients with neurotic complaints were not malingerers; he poked mild fun at doctors who were made uncomfortable by patients who did not fit into medical men's "scientific" pigeonholes. Psychologists and neurologists often declared themselves revolted by Freud's insistence that disturbed sexuality was at the root of functional nervous disorders and that sexual disturbance originated in childhood. As normal, healthy persons, they were further incensed by Freud's assertion that their motivations and some of their behavior did not essentially differ from those evident in neurotic or hysteric patients. Freud's therapeutic method, the unrestricted relation of all thoughts and feelings as they emerged, required that patients talk about what no lady could possibly discuss (and women were frequently "nervous" patients). Professor Freud indeed seemed to suggest that the middle-class decencies cost more pain than they were worth.

Yet, in spite of the initial hostility of many psychiatrists and psychologists, Freud's visit to America wakened an interest in his work that was to grow steadily during the two following decades. That growth proceeded while American society experienced an accelerating social change and might, in part at least, be attributed to the psychological impact of that change. Immediately, however, the advance of psychoanalysis in the United States was fostered by enthusiastic and energetic pioneers like James Putnam and A. A. Brill, to whose work we now turn.

[15] Jones, *op. cit.*, p. 75. The translator, Harry Chase, later became Chancellor of New York University, where Brill taught.

2 · *Forerunners and Contemporaries*

2 · Forerunners and Contemporaries

Long before James Putnam, A. A. Brill, and Trigant Burrow began their pioneer work on behalf of psychoanalysis in the United States, a number of men, often working in isolation from each other and from the mainstream of medical research, had anticipated certain Freudian insights—notably, the influence of unconscious factors and the central significance of sexuality and its distortions. Their work is all the more remarkable because they were so remote; its interest is the greater because it points toward the presence of a degree of psychological sensitivity which, once the initial barriers were lowered, may have made it easier for psychoanalysis to be popularized in the United States.

Before turning to the earliest of these students of what we now term mental or emotional disorders, it seems worth mentioning that certain American states were among the first of the world's communities to make systematic public provision for the care of the insane. Such provision at times attempted to provide treatment as well as a custody more kind than concealment in private homes or confinement in public prisons or almshouses, which was often the fate of the "deranged." During the first four decades of the nineteenth century, Americans, in the North at least, had shown a noteworthy concern in seeking better methods for dealing with the community's delinquents and defectives. They had improved prison systems, introduced programs for handling young offenders, and founded schools for educating the blind and the deaf and dumb. Largely through the determined effort of Dorothea Dix, the public conscience was aroused on behalf of people termed insane and legislatures appropriated money to set up asylums for the care of the mentally disturbed. Staffing these often became a matter of political patronage, but the existence of such institutions did give genuinely interested doctors opportunities for research. Moreover, the maintenance of insane asylums in what was still a relatively underdeveloped country indicated both medical and even lay interest in emotional disorders. Alongside fear and revulsion, there was a kind of curiosity and openness which, again, would tend to ease the way of Freudian theory once it had won initial acceptance among psychologists and psychiatrists.

A Variety of Pioneers

The first American who can be called a psychiatrist was Dr. Benjamin Rush (1745–1813), author of a treatise on diseases of the mind, published in 1812, probably the earliest such study to appear in the United States. Rush was one of the signers of the Declaration of Independence and active in organizing what limited medical service Washington's army had. Active in politics both before and after the Revolution, Rush usually stood on the "radical" side of current political debate. It seems appropriate that as a doctor, Rush should have been much in advance of his time in dealing with persons who were emotionally disturbed. He described man as "a single indivisible being"—in contradiction to prevailing religious and philosophical opinion, which considered a dichotomy between body and soul essential to understanding man as a moral being. Accordingly, Rush sought to treat the body along with the "distracted" soul, sometimes by such odd methods as strapping a patient to a chair and plunging him into cold water to frighten him out of his symptoms. However primitive his approach to psychotherapy may have been,

Rush was a good observer: James Wharton Fay goes so far as to say that he "anticipated the Freudians in the description and even the nomenclature of the phobias."[1] Even in treatment, Rush sometimes approached a "modern" method. On occasion, he asked his patients to write an account of their symptoms, a practice Nathan G. Goodman considers a form of "mental catharsis" that anticipates some of the technique of contemporary analytic therapy.[2]

A decade after Rush's death, Dr. L. W. Belden of Springfield, Massachusetts, described the case of Jane Rider, a seventeen-year-old girl from Vermont who had attracted attention by wandering about in a dreamlike condition. Some local clergymen said the girl was possessed by a demon and wanted to exorcise it in the traditional manner. Belden objected. Jane Rider was only a somnambulist, a sleepwalker whose "mind still believed in the reality of visions by which it is occupied." He cited several other cases of sleepwalking which resembled that of the Rider girl and supported his findings with reports from other doctors, including Samuel B. Woodward, first president of the American Psychiatric Association and superintendent of the State Lunatic Hospital at Worcester, Massachusetts. The element in Belden's study which seems most clearly akin to Freudian thought is his likening the shifting fancies of the insane to the vagrant movement of events in dreams.[3]

Amariah Brigham, a founder of the American Psychiatric Association, may have been better known in his profession than the Springfield doctor. Brigham concerned himself with the relationship between psychological and physiological disturbance. He was concerned especially with that prevalent American affliction, dyspepsia, which he found more wide-

---

[1] James Wharton Fay, *American Psychology before William James* (New Brunswick, N.J.: Rutgers University Press, 1939), p. 205.

[2] Nathan A. Goodman, *Benjamin Rush* (Philadelphia: University of Pennsylvania Press, 1934), p. 203.

[3] L. W. Belden, *An Account of Jane C. Rider: the Springfield Somnambulist* (Springfield, Mass.: G. and C. Merriam, 1834).

spread than his countrymen's eating habits—or their cookery
—could account for. Disordered minds, Brigham said, disturbed
the operation of the digestive system; dyspepsia was "psychosomatic" (a word he used, especially in the second edition of
his book, which was published in London in 1839).[4]

Dr. Samuel White (1777–1845) another founder of the
American Psychiatric Association, also seems to anticipate
aspects of Freudian thought. In discussing the causes of insanity, White accepted a deterministic view:

> From the cradle to the grave, man's life will be found a series
> of antecedents and consequents having a direct bearing on his
> physical and moral powers. To investigate the human mind, we
> must trace its history from its infant development, through man-
> hood, to decrepitude. It is by study of the entire man that we are
> to learn the deviations from the healthy standard, prostrating . . .
> energies and mental endowments.[5]

Much later, in 1878, another doctor, Edward H. Clarke,
professor at Harvard Medical School, had this to say about
dreams: "They are simply unconscious cerebration of that
part of the brain over which sleep has no power. Sleep affords
the opportunity, within certain limits, for the brain to act
of itself and dreams are the result."[6] It would be too much to
see in Clarke's comment an anticipation of Freud's notion of
the censor which, in sleep, became unwary and allowed re-

[4] Amariah Brigham, *Remarks on the Influence of Mental Cultivation and Mental Excitement upon Health* (Boston: March, Capen, and Lyon, 1833). Brigham wrote: "The terms *psyche* and *soma*, and *psychic* and *somatic*, both derived from the Greek, were long used independently by Italian, German, French, and English medical writers. Also combinations of these words, such as psycho-physical and psycho-organic, appear frequently in medical literature prior to the introduction of the psychosomatic by J. C. Heinroth, a German, in 1815." (See E. L. Margetts, "The Early History of the Word 'psychosomatic,'" *Canadian Medical Journal*, vol. 63, 1950.)

[5] Samuel White, "Annual Address on Insanity," *Transactions of the New York Medical Society*, Feb. 7, 1844.

[6] Edward H. Clarke, *Visions: A Study of False Sight* (Cambridge, Mass.: Houghton Osgood and Company, 1873).

pressed material to rise into awareness, but Clarke's taking dreams seriously rather than merely dismissing them is suggestive of things to come.

Perhaps the most startling likeness to the psychoanalytic approach to the origin and treatment of emotional disorders are some statements made by Andrew J. Ingersoll (1818–93) of Corning, New York. Dr. Ingersoll was intensely religious, an involvement which made him sensitive to the role sexual repression played in generating the obsessive doubts and fears which tormented so many religious patients. He recognized a causal relationship between hysterical symptoms and "the voluntary suppression of the sexual life," and made it part of his treatment to inquire into that phase of his patient's history. Ingersoll claimed that, more than once, he cured serious symptoms, such as paralysis, simply by listening to his patient's confidences and then persuading him that "since the sexual desire had been bestowed by God, it must be acceptable to man."[7]

Yet, for all these scattered examples of insight, psychological medicine did not make many advances in America before the 1890's. Psychiatrists concerned themselves with asylum management or, later, with attempts to classify mental diseases. Neurologists concentrated on the physical aspects of the nervous system. Psychologists, when they finally separated their work from philosophy, tested human perceptions and, seeking to uncover laws of learning, shut themselves up with rats or with human subjects who were trying to memorize nonsense syllables.

It is in some Utopian communities, in faith cure cults, and in literature that we find hints of the interest in emotional problems which really opened the way for psychoanalytic therapy in the United States.

Oberndorff thinks that Andrew Ingersoll may have been drawn to his insight into the relation between sexual repression

[7] A. A. Brill, "An American Precursor of Freud," *Bulletin of the New York Academy of Medicine*, XVI, No. 10, 1940.

and hysterical symptoms by acquaintance with the community at Oneida, New York, which was not too far from Corning.[8] Oneida was one among the many Utopian communities founded in the United States during the 1830's and early 1840's. All intended to teach by their example that men could organize their economic and social lives in ways better adapted to human development than those which prevailed outside. A number of them emphasized equality between men and women, allowing women to participate in community management, but Oneida was unique in its attempt to carry social reorganization into the sexual sphere. Its founder, John Humphrey Noyes (1811–86), was a man of powerful personality, an evangelist who stirred men's souls at revival meetings. He came to believe that men could attain moral perfection on earth; they did not need to wait for heaven. Such perfection was to be attained by living together, holding all things in common, and working for the general good.

Noyes and his followers, finding themselves unwelcome in Vermont, settled at Oneida in 1848 and prospered as a community: they manufactured excellent steel traps and later set up a factory for making silver-plated cutlery. Oneida succeeded where other attempts at communal living had failed because it went to the root of the matter, Noyes argued: conventional marriage—the claim of one person to permanent possession of another's love—was the basis of all selfishness and economic exploitation. Moral perfection required that people be free to love each other, that love be general, not special. Accordingly, at Oneida, mates and children, as well as goods, belonged to the community as a whole. Noyes proclaimed that the "sexual organs have a social function which is distinct from the propagative function." Sex was free, therefore; partners were changed frequently since "special" love and marriage were rejected in favor of mutual love among all Oneidans.[9] Noyes was concerned not only with improving

[8] Clarence P. Oberndorf, *Psychoanalysis in America* (New York: Grune & Stratton, 1953), p. 21.

[9] The obligation to mutual love was enforced at special weekly meet-

society but also with improving the race of man. Hence Oneidans practiced not only free love but birth control and "stirpiculture": children were begotten only with something like community permission and by persons considered peculiarly qualified to pass wisdom, talent, beauty, or strength on to their offspring.

Oneida's example aroused antagonism rather than imitation among its neighbors—who were also rather irritated by its prosperity. Threats of legal prosecution brought the community to an end in the 1870's. It had lasted for a generation, however, and many of the young people born and brought up there seem to have grown into what Abraham Maslow calls "self-realizing persons."[10]

If awareness of some relationship between the social distortion of sexuality and an unbalanced, overly competitive society be considered an anticipation of psychoanalytic insight, then the Oneida community may be seen as a precursor not only of Freud but also of Wilhelm Reich.

The important role which healing played in many of the cults that proliferated between 1830 and 1870 in the United States points toward a neglect of emotional disorders by conventionally educated physicians. Healing cults often revived the methods and some of the theory of Anton Mesmer (1733?–1815), who had performed seemingly miraculous cures by the transfer of something he called "animal magnetism" between himself and his patients. Some American healers were also familiar with Dr. James Braid's researches into hypnotism and employed the English doctor's technique in treating symptoms which would now be termed psychosomatic or even hysteric. In that respect, at least, we may consider people like Phineas Quimby (1802–1866) precursors of Freud, who also employed hypnotism before he discovered the effectiveness of free association.

---

ings when Oneidans criticized themselves and each other in something like a group therapy procedure.

[10] Abraham A. Maslow, "The Self-Actualizing Person," in Clark Moustakis, ed., *The Self: Explorations in Personal Growth* (New York: Harper, 1956), pp. 160–94.

About 1850, Quimby achieved a wide reputation for successful hypnotic treatment of a variety of physical illnesses. One
of his early patients was Mary Baker Eddy (1821–1910), whom
he cured of a convulsive disorder. As a result, Mrs. Eddy became interested in the mind's power over the body, and this
interest eventually led her to develop Christian Science. Her
system, by its general questioning of external reality and by
affording an outlet for repressed wishes, gave many mentally
troubled and physically ill believers emotional satisfaction and
solace.[11]

Literature presents something of a contrast to the general
professional indifference to psychological medicine so much
in evidence during the second half of the nineteenth century.
After Rush, instances of the kind of advanced insights we have
noted were apt to come from doctors who practiced in small
towns, whose professional education was not very broad (few
states imposed official standards or required licenses for the
practice of medicine), and whose contact with the centers of
medical science was limited. Their work, moreover, made no
great impression on the medical community. The writers Na-
thaniel Hawthorne and Oliver Wendell Holmes made far more
public stir; their work presents some startling resemblances to
Freudian theory and, in Hawthorne's case, even to Freudian
therapy.

The Scarlet Letter seemed a shockingly "impure" book to
many readers when Hawthorne published it in 1850. The
twentieth-century reader takes adultery in stride; he can accept people as good although they do what they know to be
wrong and suffer from guilt as a result. Contemporary critics,
influenced by Freud as so many of them are, often see Hawthorne himself as a man preoccupied with guilt who produced
much of his work, and this novel particularly, in order to
"write out" his own emotion, as it were, and thus to achieve a

[11] To students of the American social scene, Mrs. Eddy and Christian Science are noteworthy not only as a healing cult but also as a
faith which offered its followers a mother figure as guide instead of the
more conventional father-surrogate.

catharsis. Neither the theme of guilt nor Hawthorne's use of it
warrants our taking *The Scarlet Letter* as a true foreshadowing
of analytic thought. Yet how much suggestive material it
offers. Consider, for example, Hawthorne's description of the
doctor (the wronged husband, too, in this case) with a patient
whose body suffers, but not merely from the body's ills:

So Roger Chillingworth—the man of skill, the kind and friendly
physician—strove to go deep into his patient's bosom, delving
among his principles, prying into his recollections, and probing
everything with a cautious touch, like a treasure seeker in a dark
cavern. Few secrets escape an investigator, who has opportunity
and license to undertake such a quest, and the skill to follow it up.

Hawthorne does not approve of the doctor's intrusion into
the life of Arthur Dimmesdale's soul, but few modern observers have described the practice of therapy so neatly. And
again, see Hawthorne's remarkable presentation of the pas-
sivity of the doctor, another aspect of classical psychoanalytic
technique:

If the physician possess native sagacity, and a nameless something more—let us call it intuition; if he shows no intrusive egotism
nor disagreeably prominent characteristics of his own; if he has
the power, which must be born with him, to bring his mind into
such affinity with his patient's, that this last shall unawares have
spoken what he imagines himself only to have thought; if such
revelations be received without tumult, and acknowledged not so
often by an uttered sympathy as by silence, and inarticulate breath,
and here and there a word, to indicate that all is understood; if
to these qualifications of a confidant be joined all the advantages
afforded by his recognized character as a physician—then, at some
inevitable moment, will the soul of the sufferer be dissolved, and
flow forth in a dark but transparent stream, bringing all its mys-
teries into the daylight.

In the continuation of this description of the relationship between doctor and patient, one can find indications of both the
positive transference and the resistance which a contemporary
psychotherapist encounters.

Many of Hawthorne's short stories, too, repay study in the light of psychoanalytic concepts, but such study is not our purpose here. We are concerned only to point out that the continuing interest which Hawthorne's work had for certain American readers shows a sensitivity to psychological problems which would later predispose other Americans to accept psychoanalysis as something beyond a medical specialty.

Few familiar with Oliver Wendell Holmes's poems and essays think of him as a doctor. Physician he was, however, and professor of anatomy at Harvard. His essay on childbed fever might have saved lives and suffering if it had inspired doctors to greater cleanliness when they delivered babies, but there is small evidence that it exerted much influence. Perhaps that accounts for his presenting his psychological observations to the receptive readers of novels rather than to his unresponsive fellow professionals.[12]

In 1870, Holmes delivered before the Harvard chapter of Phi Beta Kappa a lecture that actually discusses the operation of the unconscious. Free association and its mechanism is quite literally described:

The more we examine the mechanism of thought, the more we shall see that the automatic, unconscious action of the mind enters largely into all its processes. Our definite ideas are stepping stones; how we get from one to the other, we do not know; something carries us; we do not take the step.

Later in the same paper, Holmes seems even closer to the *Psychopathology of Everyday Life*, saying:

We wish to remember something in the course of conversation.

[12] Clarence P. Oberndorf, *The Psychiatric Novels of Oliver Wendell Holmes* (New York: Columbia University Press, 1945). In *Elsie Venner*, Holmes presents a schizophrenic girl; he tells the story of an hysterical adolescent in *The Guardian Angel* and describes the psychic factors in allergies in *A Mortal Antipathy*, which also shows the influence of neurotic fear of women in a young man. None of these stories has much literary merit, but all are interesting as fictionalized case histories, presenting material not unlike some of that encountered in contemporary practice.

No effort of the will can reach it; but we say, "Wait a minute, and it will come to me," and go on talking. Presently, perhaps some minutes later, the idea we are in search of comes all at once into the mind, delivered like a prepaid bundle, laid at the door of consciousness like a foundling in a basket. How it came there we know not.[13]

Whether Holmes applied his insights to the treatment of patients we do not really know. It is likely that teaching and writing left him rather little time for practice. His novels were far less read than his urbane essays, and his Phi Beta Kappa address does not seem to have had any noticeable impact on the educated public.

The nervous patient and "neurasthenia" became more familiar during the 1880's. Some doctors suspected psychological factors to be operative, but no systematic psychological treatment was used. Louisa May Alcott shows a fictional doctor curing a "nervous" young girl by loosening her stays and prescribing vigorous exercise.[14] S. Weir Mitchell, a doctor who produced fiction (none of it concerned with the study of character) established a reputation for treating nervous patients with rest and special diet.

To summarize: at the end of the nineteenth century, doctors were aware of emotional disorders; they were interested in describing mental disturbances and developing diagnostic categories, but they felt rather helpless to devise effective treatment. A new flare of interest in hypnosis had appeared, particularly as practiced by the Swiss Auguste Forel, but that too proved disappointing. One kind of treatment after another —water cures, rest cures, diet cures—became the medical fashion and dropped into obscurity.

By 1909, then, American doctors confronted with patients who had hysterical symptoms or psychosomatic complaints

---

[13] Oliver Wendell Holmes, *Pages from an Old Volume of Life*, "Mechanism in Thought and Morals; an address delivered before the Phi Beta Kappa Society of Harvard University, June 29, 1870," pp. 260-314.
[14] Louisa May Alcott, *Eight Cousins* (Boston: Bird Richards, 1874).

would, if they spoke frankly, admit that their regimens and their drugs were no more reliably effective than the rituals of the faith healers and cultists they despised. Again, factors in the American social situation were preparing the ground for the acceptance of Freudian theory and analytic therapy.

James Jackson Putnam

It was at this point that certain American contemporaries of Freud became acquainted with his work and proceeded to bring it before the public, medical and lay. Three particularly interesting figures among these pioneers are James Jackson Putnam, A. A. Brill, and Trigant Burrow.

Putnam (1846–1918) was the most generally known of the three in 1909. He had taken advanced training in Europe after the Civil War and had become a specialist in neurology; he was first to teach that subject at the Harvard Medical School. Because of his reputation as a neurologist he was often called as an expert witness in cases involving neuroses occurring as the result of physical injury. Such litigation occurred more frequently after 1890 as the states adopted laws providing that workmen be compensated for injuries received on the job. Putnam had an unusual capacity for recognizing the actuality of neurotic suffering, whether physically precipitated or not, and was unusually aware of the relationship between neurosis and social circumstances, an awareness that gave him a particular concern with what we should now call mental health.

About 1904 or 1905 Putnam first became interested in psychoanalysis; in December, 1909, he published the earliest adequate account of Freud's work to appear in English.[15] He was not entirely convinced of its therapeutic value, and continued

[15] "Personal Impressions of Sigmund Freud and his Work," *Journal of Abnormal Psychology*, December, 1909. Reprinted in J. J. Putnam, *Addresses on Psycho-Analysis* (London: Hogarth Press, 1951), pp. 1–30.

to employ hypnosis in treatment. Gradually, however, as Putnam pursued his study of psychoanalysis, he became more and more convinced of its value. He defended its searching of the patient's past, including past sexuality, against those who called such inquiry "unwholesome, unhealthy, morbid." "Knowledge," he insisted, "knows nothing as essentially dirty."[16] He defended the scientific character of Freud's theory, noting how, when one of his own cases seemed to contradict Freud, deeper probing found ". . . underneath the faults and failings, the fears and habits of adult life . . . the workings out of the instinctive cravings of imaginative, pleasure-seeking, and pain-shunning infancy, dragging back the adult from the fulfillment of his higher destiny." He emphasized, too, the wide relevance of psychoanalysis and the social emphasis of analytic treatment. Consider what he told the New York Harvey Society, a medical group, in the fall of 1911:

On the other hand, it is not just to characterize psychoanalysis solely as a therapeutic measure. In proportion as the psychoanalytic movement has developed toward maturity, it has shown itself able to make scientific contributions of great value to psychiatry, psychology, mythology, philology, sociology, as well as to education and to prophylaxis. In other words, these investigations bring support to every research which deals with the inward and the outward manifestations of human effort and mental evolution, while at the same time they draw important aid from all these inquiries into the psychology of the human race, for the benefit of the single human life.

The practical aim of this method is to enable persons who are hampered by nervous symptoms and faults of character to make themselves more efficient members of society by teaching them to shake themselves free from the subtle web of delusive, misleading, half-unconscious ideas by which they are bound and blinded as if through the influence of an evil spell. Such persons—and in some measure the statement is true of all persons—have to learn that they are responsible, not only for the visible but also for the hid-

[16] *Ibid.*, p. 18.

den portions of themselves, and that, hard as the task may be, they should learn to know themselves thoroughly in this sense. For it is the whole of ourselves which acts. . . .[17]

Again and again, as Putnam explained psychoanalysis to psychologists and neurologists and defended it against charges that it was unscientific, prurient, and socially dangerous, he insisted that knowledge would make for health. His reiteration that psychoanalysis was an educative procedure which made it possible for people to control their instincts effectively, rather than a polysyllabic apology for loose living, may well have made psychoanalysis acceptable to a people already willing to treat education as a magic key to social and individual progress.[18]

As differences developed between Freud and his former followers, Jung and Adler, Putnam took Freud's side. This is the more remarkable because Freud and his group were not at all sympathetic to Putnam's contention that psychoanalysis would not achieve true maturity until it set itself into an appropriate philosophic context,[19] divorced itself from what is called "scientism" nowadays, and recognized the claims of intuition. Putnam's view, incidentally, seems to be winning a good deal of support in recent decades. Some psychotherapists are concerned lest widespread familiarity with psychoanalysis tend to deplete the individual's sense of responsibility. Others, feeling that their patients are suffering less from too stringent a body of social imperatives than from a sense of being without goals and without identity, have turned to versions of existentialism, for instance, in order to supply the philosophic frame of reference whose lack Putnam noted forty-odd years ago.

[17] *Ibid.*, pp. 80, 100.
[18] Freud, of course, thought of psychoanalysis as the contrary of education, in an instructional sense, since the analyst was passive and nondirective.
[19] Ernest Jones, "Dr. James Jackson Putnam; Human Motives," *International Journal of Psycho-Analysis*, I, 1920, pp. 328–29. See also, Putnam, *op. cit.*, pp. 79–96.

A. A. Brill

Putnam was a transmitter and a defender of Freudian theory; some of his statements are suggestive of aspects of post-Freudian thought, but he did not contribute much to theory before he died. Abraham A. Brill (1874–1948) filled much the same sort of role. Brill's main service to psychoanalysis in the United States was as translator, organizer, and popularizer on a relatively high level. He was educated as a physician and underwent psychoanalytic training at Zurich. In our time, when analytic training has been formalized (in part as a result of Brill's own effort), it seems strange to read his description of the work at Burghölzli:

> We all read Freud's work on dreams, his and Breuer's book on hysterics, and his book on sex. The only easy and interesting reading were the case records and some of the papers on the neuroses. Everything else had to be studied [at first hand] usually with the help of those who had considerable experience in analysis.[20]

In 1911, two years after Freud's visit, Brill organized the New York Psychoanalytic Society. As a result of Brill's work as a translator, Americans unfamiliar with German could read the *Three Contributions to the Theory of Sex* (1910) and *The Interpretation of Dreams* (1913). The translator's task is never easy, but Brill's was truly formidable: he had to choose English words which would convey the special technical significance Freud was giving his German.[21] And he had to make his choice in the knowledge that the terms he selected might well become the basic vocabulary of a new discipline. Brill's translations have been adversely criticized, and they have been partially superseded by more modern, accurate, and graceful

[20] A. A. Brill, "The Introduction and Development of Freud's Work in the United States," *American Journal of Sociology*, 1938, p. 318*n*.

[21] Freud is considered a master of German prose—he received the Goethe prize, it will be remembered—but he made his language serve his thought, not the convenience of translators.

versions. Yet Brill's work served psychoanalysis well. He dared
to make Freud speak English when others trying to acquaint
the English-speaking world with psychoanalysis still left
Freud's crucial terms in German.

Trigant Burrow

Brill never faltered in Freudian orthodoxy. Psychoanalysis
was what Freud had made it, and he saw no reason to move
from the master's ground. Trigant Burrow (1875–1950) was
less rigid. He was one of the few analysts who rather consistently kept sociological factors in the foreground of his
attention. His readiness to make innovations in analytic technique led Burrow to become one of the founders of group
psychotherapy, an important phase of contemporary clinical
practice. Unlike Putnam and Brill, Burrow was American
trained. He studied medicine at the University of Virginia and
went on to take a doctorate in psychology at Johns Hopkins.
His interest in emotional disorder was awakened by work in
a philosophy seminar when his teacher declared that none of
the leading European psychiatrists had yet " 'ignited the spark'
requisite to bring about understanding of the basic cause of
mental disease. . . . I remember that I then and there recorded
the pledge to devote my life's work to the effort to contribute
what I could towards igniting this spark. . . ."[22]

Burrow did his first work under the well-known American
psychiatrist, Adolf Meyer. When Freud and Jung came to the
United States, Burrow was introduced to them. Although
Meyer was not especially enthusiastic about Freudian theory,
he encouraged Burrow to study it further and to become an
analysand himself. Burrow studied with Jung in Zurich, became increasingly enthusiastic, and returned to begin analytic
practice on his own, the second man in America to do so, and

---

[22] Trigant Burrow, *A Search for Man's Sanity: The Selected Letters
of Trigant Burrow* (New York: Oxford University Press, 1958), p. 17.

the first of American birth.[23] Burrow was not unsatisfied with his own preparation, yet he arranged to begin an analysis with Freud, which was prevented, however, by World War I.

Thereafter, although Burrow continued his interest in psychoanalysis and kept in touch with Freud, he tended more and more to change his focus. As he wrote his old chief, Adolf Meyer: "I have been trying to state in writing as clearly as I can what seems to me the basic occasion of the failure of analysis—our exclusive emphasis of the personal to the utter neglect of inherent social factors." He became more and more interested in group behavior because he was convinced that, since men are always part of social groups, analysis of the individual and his problems cannot be completed without thorough study of the group. Burrow devised a technique of group analysis which is doubtless one of his most significant contributions to psychotherapy in America.

In the 1940's, Burrow felt that his contribution had been slighted. He had been the true pioneer in the area the neo-Freudians were then exploring. At the end of the decade, he wrote rather acrimoniously: "I have not myself read either Fromm or Horney, but a good many people have spoken of what they felt was the tendency of these authors to borrow rather freely from my thesis. Harry Stack Sullivan helped himself lavishly to my material. I knew him at Hopkins and he received through the years all of my reprints."[24]

The Shock of Novelty

If Burrow felt his work unfairly neglected by his contemporaries, he was experiencing a fate frequently encountered by intellectual pioneers. Certainly the early proponents of psychoanalysis in America found themselves attacked from

[23] *Ibid.*, pp. 30–31.
[24] *Ibid.*, pp. 38, 78; see also Burrow, "Psychoanalytic Improvisations and the Personal Equation," *Psychoanalytic Review*, XIII (1926), p. 173.

many sides. Some academic psychologists, including Hugo
Munsterberg of Harvard, denied that the unconscious existed.
Others, like J. J. Jastrow, wrote about that phase of the psyche
as if Freud's work had not been done.[25] Brill tells how he
lectured to a gathering of economists and sociologists (he does
not name the group nor give a date to the episode) who
listened to him with interest but because he cited cases to show
the sexual factor at work beneath some people's opposition to
social authority, he was found unworthy to write an article on
the relationship between psychoanalysis and sociology.[26]

It was even difficult for Brill to find an American publisher
for his translations of Freud. Dr. Smith Ely Jelliffe published
the *Three Contributions to the Theory of Sex* in the series of
monographs he edited,[27] but Brill had to go to England to find
a publisher who would risk bringing out *The Psychopathology
of Everyday Life* or *The Interpretation of Dreams.*

The public sometimes seemed less squeamish than the professionals. Certain sociologists, particularly in the Middle West
and on the Pacific Coast, were more open to Freudian thought
before World War I than were some psychologists. To conventional academic psychologists, struggling to win status as
a science for their discipline, psychoanalysis seemed "unscientific" because it was not amenable to either statistical inquiry
or to controlled experimentation. And no label could be more
insulting.

Psychoanalysis might have been expected to remain alien to
psychology even longer than it did. Yet ultimately, few aspects
of psychology escaped Freudian influence, largely because of
outside pressure—awareness of psychoanalysis among the general public and demands of students to learn more about it.
Shakow and Rapoport even suggest that psychologists them-

[25] Celia Burns Stendler, "New Ideas for Old: How Freudianism Was
Received in the United States," *Journal of Educational Psychology*,
XXXVIII, No. 4 (1947), p. 196.

[26] Brill, *op. cit.*, p. 321.

[27] For the Nervous and Mental Disease Publication Company of New
York.

selves were suffering from a sense of guilt: they recognized an obligation to contribute to men's usable knowledge of themselves and realized that much of their work, even in learning theory, did not help people understand their own behavior.[28]

Brill, meantime, continued his effort to win psychoanalysis a wider hearing. He lectured to lay groups as well as to professionals. He addressed the ladies of the Child Study Association on "a very delicate subject," masturbation. He talked to the Authors League. A "young man named Walter Lippmann" introduced him to Mabel Dodge.[29] Mrs. Dodge received all the interesting people in America in her salon that winter of 1913; artists, writers, philosophers, militant unionists gathered there, exchanged ideas, argued, planned demonstrations in support of strikers, found and lost their loves, and enjoyed seeing themselves as the most advanced of emancipated Americans. Lincoln Steffens recalled the impression which their first encounter with psychoanalysis made on Mrs. Dodge and her guests: ". . . there were no warmer, quieter, more intensely thoughtful conversations at Mabel Dodge's than those on Freud and his implications."[30]

The first really popular presentation of Freud came two years later, in 1915, when *Good Housekeeping* magazine printed Peter MacFarlane's article about Freud. It is interesting to see that it was a journal addressed to housewives rather than the *Atlantic*, or *Harper's*, or one of the more radical weeklies that brought Freud to the lay reader. However, MacFarlane carefully avoided any allusion to sex. Foreshadowing distortions to come, he presented psychoanalysis as a kind of magic cure for emotional and even physical illness.[31]

Before leaving the precursors and pioneers of psychoanalysis

---

[28] David Shakow and David Rapoport, "The Influence of Freud on American Psychology," *Psychological Issues*, Monograph 13 (1964), pp. 82–95.

[29] Brill, *op. cit.*, p. 322.

[30] Lincoln Steffens, *Autobiography* (New York: Harcourt, Brace, 1931).

[31] Peter MacFarlane, "Diagnosis by Dreams," *Good Housekeeping*, 60 (February-March, 1915), 125–33; 278–86.

in America, two conditions should be noted. The American Psychoanalytic Association, founded in 1911, did not establish its influence over the professional practice of psychoanalysis until the middle 1920's. Maintaining proper standards of qualification was no easy task, therefore, and quacks may well have flourished. Secondly, the schismatic tendencies in psychoanalysis soon became as evident in the United States as in Europe. Jung and Adler had their followers. Trigant Burrow, as has been mentioned, divorced himself from orthodoxy. His observations led him to the conclusion that "normality" in the behavioral field did not represent "a basic criterion of health comparable to that existing in other branches of medicine." Statistical norms, in other words, might merely reflect unhealthy social conditions; in a meaningful sense, society itself might be sick.[32]

Quite early in the nineteenth century, some Americans had shown an awareness of unconscious and even of sexual factors in emotional life which gave promise that a new approach to emotional problems might be welcomed when it should appear. The intuitive grasp of unconscious elements in human behavior evident in Hawthorne's novels and in the fiction of Oliver Wendell Holmes was further indication of possible American receptivity for a new interpretation of man's emotions. The overall development of American society, and particularly the restive, questioning mood of many Americans in the decade before the First World War—a mood reflected by the appearance of pragmatism in philosophy, by the growth of socialism, by the revolt against political machines, by the rebellious assertiveness of labor groups like the I.W.W., by the parades and demands of the suffragettes—again indicated that the ground had been prepared for innovation. When Freud's American contemporaries first introduced his work to the United States it met angry rejection, as might be expected. But their persistence and skill in emphasizing the potential contribution of psychoanalysis to social improvement, or at least

[32] Burrow, *A Search for Man's Sanity*, p. 42.

its potential contribution to greater understanding of the reasons that man and society were so difficult to improve, won psychoanalysis a hearing among students of society as well as among physicians. Writers and journalists became interested, too. As therapy, psychoanalysis met the needs of patients who suffered without organic cause. As theory, it offered a fuller picture of man's emotional development. Gradually during the four decades after 1909 the work of the pioneers was rewarded. Psychoanalysis became acceptable; it grew in influence; from a radical, slightly gamy novelty, it finally has become something of a commonplace, an orthodoxy in its own right facing attack from biologists who hope to find chemical reasons and remedies for neurotic behavior and from social organizers who hope to make industrial society a source of support instead of a breeding ground of tension.

3 · Popularization and the Patient

3 · Popularization and the Patient

PSYCHOANALYSIS has become accepted in the United States as a method for treating emotionally disturbed persons and as a theory contributing to our understanding of human behavior. Physicians, sociologists, anthropologists, psychologists —all have found Freud's ideas useful in deepening their knowledge of their own specialties. Novelists, playwrights, poets, painters, and sculptors have found Freud illuminating.

In consequence of this acceptance, knowledge of psychoanalysis has filtered down to many segments of the American public. The first Americans to encounter Freud were the professionals—psychologists and physicians interested in disorders of the mind. Putnam and Brill were among Freud's earliest American popularizers, and they were followed by numerous others. Indeed, by 1932, Mark Sullivan, describing the "moral dissolution" which he said characterized the 1920's, cited as evidence the couple of hundred books about Freud and psychoanalysis published since 1910.[1] Some of these were unauthorized, like André Tridon's *Psychoanalysis, Sleep, and Dreams* (1921); others, like Joseph Jastrow's *The House That Freud Built* (1932) claimed to be more serious, although they

[1] Tridon's unorthodoxy was a source of trouble to the members of the New York Psychoanalytic Society, some of whom charged him with bringing down cries of "quackery" on the whole psychoanalytic movement. (See Ruitenbeek, *The Seven Rings: Freud's Circle*, which is to appear in 1966 or 1967.) See also Mark Sullivan, *Our Times: The United States 1900–1914*, vol. IV (New York: Scribner's, 1932), pp. 166–73.

did not even pretend to have a first-hand acquaintance with Freud's own work.[2] The academic community encountered psychoanalysis in the discussions of college teachers of sociology, philosophy, and the like (academic psychology was not at this time especially receptive and in the present decade still retains some of its reservations). Outside the colleges and the universities, intellectuals encountered Freud in literary criticism, drama, and fiction. In 1912 for instance, A. B. Kuttner, a member of the staff of the influential magazine *Seven Arts*, engaged Walter Lippmann in discussion about psychoanalysis (which Kuttner had experienced as a patient as well as an interested reader); and he helped Brill translate Freud's *Interpretation of Dreams*.[3]

Transmission in Art

Plays and novels presented psychoanalysis to a general audience. Freudian theory, which brought the psychological dynamisms into the light, challenged writers to deal not with the mere surface of behavior but with the depths of emotion which give rise to that behavior. During the 1920's Eugene O'Neill made the most explicit use possible of Freudian thinking in the drama. He tried in *Strange Interlude* to put man's constant inner dialogue with himself on the stage and to show, by having his characters talk to themselves while conversing with one another, how a person may speak only to hide what he is thinking. The play attracted large, curious audiences when first presented, but it does not wear particularly well. Neither does *Mourning Becomes Electra*, where O'Neill follows the Freudian pattern of interpreting human conduct as he moves the

[2] David Shakow and David Rapoport, *The Influence of Freud on American Psychology* (New York: *Psychological Issues*, Monograph 13, 1964), p. 57.

[3] *Ibid.*, p. 59n, citing a letter of Walter Lippmann to Frederick J. Hoffman, author of *Freudianism and the Literary Mind*.

persons of the Greek legend into mid-nineteenth-century New England and there shows mother and daughter at death grips for the same man.

Lesser dramatists have followed O'Neill in using the psycho-analytic approach. In our day, only the most superficial—or the most daring—playwright would put people into action on the stage without giving some indication of familiarity with Freud's interpretation of human motives.

Novelists like Stephen Crane and Theodore Dreiser did not know Freud's work when they began to present their characters more freely and fully than had been customary in American fiction. Neither, for that matter, did Sherwood Anderson when he described some of his young writer friends beguiled by their discovery of psychoanalysis.[4] He did not need to know Freud at first hand, or second, in order to show how the attempt to suppress awareness of sexuality can warp human life. Psychoanalytic theory offers guidelines to understanding Anderson's work, however, even as it can help one appreciate a writer like Faulkner who, though seeming remote from contemporary intellectual preoccupations, might have written differently had psychoanalysis not percolated through American intellectual life.

A poet novelist like Conrad Aiken shows more direct evidence of Freud's influence. He was intellectually aware of psychoanalysis (indeed, Freud offered Aiken a period in treatment with him, so impressed was he with the character of the novelist's work), and he used Freudian concepts as a means of integrating his individual vision of the world. His story "Secret Snow, Silent Snow" is regarded as clinically accurate in its description of the onset of a schizophrenic episode; it is of even greater interest as a dramatization of the desire to retreat from the world; Aiken's child protagonist becomes a symbol for the rejection of contemporary existence, which is to be found in so many forms in the works of a number of

---

[4] Sherwood Anderson, *Sherwood Anderson's Memoirs* (New York: Harcourt Brace, 1942), p. 243.

contemporary American novelists. Aiken is peculiarly subtle in his use of psychoanalytic ideas to present the novelist's pursuit of experience, moving down, from the surface behavior he describes into the depths until he touches the very roots of his characters' development into the personalities he depicts.

O'Neill and Aiken are cited here as instances only; any detailed tracing of the relationship between psychoanalysis and literature in America would require several long books.[5] Through various kinds of fiction, however, the influence of Freudian thought continued to filter down, until, in the 1960's, even the poorly educated had heard of "complexes" and "repressions." Today Broadway comedies, second-rate movies, mediocre TV programs, all use psychoanalytic terms and concepts although they seek "the common touch." One can tell jokes about psychoanalysis to unselected audiences; and there is a market for comic songs about analysts, analysis, and people beguiled and bewildered by both.

In short, psychoanalysis has been thoroughly popularized. So high a degree of popularization presents both advantages and dangers. The advantages lie in the creation of an open-minded, even receptive, attitude to psychoanalytic insights and psychoanalytic therapy. Americans, as has been pointed out in other connections, have been and are still more willing than Europeans to apply Freudian concepts in the rearing and education of children, in dealing with delinquents, and in attempting to cope with their everyday problems. In some sectors of American society at least, the result has been a freer and more humane attitude toward themselves and toward the behavior of others. Because psychoanalysis has become popular ("being analyzed" has at times reached the level of fad and status symbol), Americans are comparatively willing to seek psychological counseling and even psychotherapy. In Europe, many people regard psychoanalysis as equivalent to the treatment of mental disease; hence going into analysis means that one is severely disturbed. We find few Europeans turning, as

---

[5] Frederick J. Hoffman, *Freudianism and the Literary Mind* (New York: Grove Press, 1959) is one good book-length treatment.

do a fairly large number of middle-class Americans, to psycho-analytic treatment in order "to find themselves." Perhaps fewer Europeans feel the need of special help in making that dis-covery; European society, where economic and technological changes occur more slowly than they do in the United States, gives the individual more time in which to change as his so-ciety changes.

Some Costs of Diffusion

As useful as the popularization of psychoanalysis has been, it has also often entailed a high degree of misunderstanding of Freud and, more important perhaps, a measure of harm to per-sons who have suffered because popularizations have given them misleading ideas about psychotherapy. The damaging effects of popularization may be briefly categorized as vulgar-ization, dilution, and distortion. Freud himself found his satis-faction in the American receptivity to psychoanalysis dimmed because he thought that did not mean wide or deep knowledge of his work. Even professional therapists preferred to "shorten study and preparation [and] proceed as fast as possible to prac-tical application"; hence they were apt to study not from the "original sources, but from second-hand and often inferior accounts." Americans, as he wrote in his introduction to a special number of *The Medical Review of Reviews,* had made few really new contributions to the theory of psychoanalysis. Those who used it in therapy showed "little interest in its scientific problems and its cultural significance." The catch-words of analysis were known, not its meaning.

Thus, Freud's sexual theory has been vulgarized into a per-missive, even encouraging, attitude toward promiscuity. His concept of the conflict between Eros and Thanatos, between adult love and the drive toward self-destructive behavior, has been vulgarized into "love will solve all problems"—with *love* defined as a kind of non-discriminating, sentimental acceptance. Through such vulgarization, notions derived from some of

Freud's writings have been used to give platitudes at least an aroma of relevance to contemporary problems.

The dilution of Freud's ideas exists on a somewhat different level from what is called their vulgarization. Here one sees an attempt to adapt a rather harsh view of human existence to a tradition which may be summarized in the phrase of the nine-teenth-century novelist, William Dean Howells: "the smiling aspects of life are the more American." It may indeed seem unfair to apply the term *dilution* to the serious studies which modify Freud's grim picture of the price men must pay for their existence in human culture. Among these studies, the work of neo- and post-Freudian scholars like Erich Fromm and Erik Erikson is of particular significance. Fromm's early studies, like those of Erikson, treat culture, i.e., life in what we know as civilization, as natural to man. Where Freud em-phasizes the necessary deprivations imposed by culture, these scholars stress culture as a means of fulfillment. Where he, like Rousseau, sees the restriction on the expression of instinctual drives, they see the potentialities of life in civilization. Such a modification of the Freudian attitude (see pp. 105–120, for a detailed discussion) toward man's plight might better be called development than dilution, except, of course, from the point of view of a rigidly orthodox Freudian.

More validly described as dilution are certain changes some analysts have rung upon Freud's insistence that emotional health requires men to recognize and accept reality. The psy-choanalytic maxim that one achieves maturity by learning to accept reality and to live by its requirements has been trans-lated into a new sanction for social conformity. Psychoanaly-sis is said to support the demand that the patient "adjust" to the contemporary world. Desire for social change is said to express only rebelliousness and immaturity. It would be unfair to charge this version of psychotherapy with responsibility for the complacency which characterized so much American thinking in the social sciences during the 1950's, but the "ad-justment ideal" in therapy has certainly done nothing to counteract complacency.

A third type of dilution of Freudian theory has operated to gloss over Freud's atheism and, going further, to transform psychoanalytic concepts into a basis for religious orthodoxy. This dilution has been extraordinarily successful (see pp. 93–120).

Distortion of Freud's theory has occurred less because some of its elements and attitudes were unacceptable than because of attempts to simplify a subtle, complex set of concepts which changed as they developed over a long period of time. Other kinds of distortion have occurred as a result of effort to adapt psychoanalytic concepts to the preconceptions of religious groups, as a result of rigid application of Freud's technical methods, and, ironically, as the result of attempts to spread the benefits of psychotherapy. Patients too often come into treatment with exaggerated and highly unrealistic expectations in consequence of the misconceptions they have absorbed. Even therapists are uncertain, in some such instances, about what progress is possible in the course of therapy, so much debris must be cleared away before real work in treatment can begin.

One specific way in which Freud has been distorted is the notion that *any* repression is bad and has harmful consequences; hence the child should not only be allowed to express all its natural desires but also have them gratified so far as law permits. Similar is the distortion involved in the equation of Freudian psychological theory and sexual permissiveness: because emotional disturbance can be traced to disturbance in the progress of sexual development, Freud's misinterpreters argue that selectivity in choosing sexual partners (let alone restraint in sexual behavior) is psychologically unhealthy.

Misinterpretation of this sort was common during the 1920's and has not entirely disappeared. In the decade after the First World War, however, Freud was blamed for all the evils of the jazz age, from the murder of young Gerald Frank by Leopold and Loeb to the inadequacy of the contemporary novel. It was Maxwell Bodenheim—whose death was at least partly caused by a disorderly sex life—who protested that people who accepted Freud really wanted only to talk and think about sex. Aldous Huxley called Freudian dream interpretation "obscene."[6]

As we saw earlier, Freud's scientific emphasis on sexuality sparked much of the professional opposition which his work encountered. It may have been just that same emphasis that made Freudian theory particularly acceptable to young American writers, who wanted greater freedom to express their experience of themselves and of the characters they created. Hoffman's study, *Freudianism and the Literary Mind*, cites Sherwood Anderson's description of the way in which the writers who gathered about Floyd Dell (an important figure in the twenties, although now all but forgotten as a novelist) set about "psyching" each other, using Jung's word association tests, watching each other's slips of tongue and gesture, and engaging in glib chatter about "repression." Like other less creative Americans, Dell and his friends used psychoanalysis as a fresh excuse to talk about themselves. Anderson remarked that he was completely unfamiliar with Freud when he entered the Dell circle (and never did, in fact, read any of Freud's books), "and was rather ashamed" of his ignorance. Dell ". . . had begun psyching us. Not Floyd alone but others in the group did it. They psyched me. They psyched men passing in the street. It was a time when it was well for a man to be somewhat guarded in the remarks he made, what he did with his hands."[7]

Such conversion of psychoanalysis into parlor small talk has continued since the 1920's. But psychoanalytic terms, usually misunderstood, are now used not only by intellectuals and rebellious young writers like those Sherwood Anderson described, but also by middle-class housewives and even by quite uneducated people who have seen "psychological" films or read books and magazine articles with titles like "how psychoanalysis stopped me from eating myself fat" or "how psychotherapy brought me back to God and free enterprise."

[6] Maxwell Bodenheim, "Psychoanalysis and American Fiction," *Nation*, CXIV (1922), p. 684.

[7] Anderson, *op. cit.*, p. 244.

Another distortion of Freud and psychoanalysis involves such problems as the responsibility of individuals for their actions and of validity of "values," *i.e.*, the problem of moral imperatives and sanctions. Because unconscious factors have been found to be so important in determining attitudes, opinions, and actions, it is said that psychoanalysis warrants the contention that no person can justly be held to account for anything he does. Because psychoanalytic theory shows that much of what is called *conscience* is actually the superego—the internalized commands of the culture as those are mediated and passed on to children through the attitudes, and the possible neuroses, of parents—it is said that psychoanalysis has destroyed all moral authority and all effective ethical sanctions.

These distortions are sufficiently prevalent, incidentally, to spark a running and often intense controversy between one group of psychoanalysts who insist that they are concernd with treatment and treatment alone, and therefore cannot properly be concerned with the value systems of their patients or with the unexpressed basic premises of society, and another group who insist that, for some of their patients at least, the absence of viable values actually constitutes a large part of their illness.

Such distortions offer evidence that, although analytic therapy is acceptable in the United States and terms drawn from psychoanalysis in general use, Freud and his writings are not really well known in America. Even the abridgment of Ernest Jones' monumental biography is too long for the impatient reader and requires too much knowledge from the person with no previous grounding in psychoanalytic theory. Short biographical treatments of Freud by people who knew him are available, but those, unfortunately, are often too colored by their authors' opinions to have either objectivity or adequate scope. One can scarcely blame the public for being unreceptive to the numerous exercises in sectarian disputation which have been termed lives, or at least reminiscences, of Freud. Yet even Martin Freud's charming biography of his father has had small attention.

If Freud the man is insufficiently known, Freud the philosophical psychologist is as little or less known and this despite
the fact that most of his major theoretical work is available
in inexpensive form. Educated laymen are not generally familiar with even *Moses and Monotheism* or *Civilization and Its
Discontents*. *Beyond the Pleasure Principle* and *Group Psychology and the Analysis of the Ego* are even less read, although large numbers of copies may be bought. Professional
analysts themselves tend to concentrate on vocationally useful
texts and to ignore Freud's own work. This is particularly
apparent among peripheral practitioners such as counselors,
social workers, and the like, who, increasingly aware of their
clients' need for psychotherapy, try to act as therapists although they may lack full training. The tendency to depend
on commentaries, expositions, and the like also is shown by
some who are preparing to make psychotherapy their life's
work. Indeed, one observer has remarked that the American
psychoanalyst is often a kind of "night-school" professional,
so busy earning the cost of his own training that he has no
time to make that training either broad or deep.[8]

If professionals are thus ill-informed about Freud and his
ideas, the lay public is too frequently misinformed. The shallow character of certain books designed to convey some of
Freud's thought to the general reader has contributed to misinformation.[9] Another source of misunderstanding among the
uninformed is the clamorous presence of the various schools
of psychoanalytic thought. Here, discussion may be on either
a professional or a more general level, but it often tends to be
acrimonious rather than enlightening. One might cite journals
like *The Psychoanalytic Quarterly* and *The Journal of the
American Psychoanalytic Association*, which present by and
large the Freudian viewpoint; *Psychiatry* and the *Review of
Existential Psychology and Psychiatry*, which serve as a forum

[8] Shakow and Rapoport, *op. cit.*, pp. 68–70.
[9] James Chaplin, *The Unconscious* (New York: Ballantine Books,
1960); Sanford Beyer, *Each Man Kills* (New York: Ballantine Books,
1962) are good examples.

for neo-Freudians like Erich Fromm and Rollo May. The untutored reader may well be bewildered—although if he persists, he may penetrate the quarreling to reach the insights that lie behind disputation. The reader who limits himself to more popular books is apt to acquire nothing beyond a smattering of jargon which makes him think he knows something about psychoanalysis when he has only a new set of words for his ignorance.

Books like Louis Busch's *Be Glad You're Neurotic* or Lucy Freeman's *Hope for the Troubled*, for example, may be well intentioned enough. Certainly, they avoid the sensationalism of such work as A. K. Daniel's *It's Never too Late to Love* or Howard Whitman's *Let's Tell the Truth about Sex*. Nor do they suggest, with S. Pickworth Farrow, that you *Psycho-analyze Yourself* or, with E. Oakly, that you acquire *Self-Confidence through Self-Analysis*. But even the more sober books contribute to distortion: in order to be interesting, they present their material in a fashion that leads some readers to think of psychoanalysis as an easy enterprize relatively free of boredom and demanding little effort, where the euphoria that a patient may feel at the beginning of therapy never flags and where the process of self-discovery is a continuously thrilling experience.

Sometimes the distortion is primarily the work of marketers, the persons who write titillating captions, invent titles which promise pornography (*Twilight Women*, for instance), or jacket a solid piece of writing like Eric Berne's *Layman's Guide to Psychiatry and Psychoanalysis* with a picture of a young woman with languorous, painted eyelids offering her sensually parted lips to the beholder.

Psychoanalysis in the Mass Media

Popularization often takes the shape of newspaper columns and TV programs. These columnists (Dr. Rose Franzblau in the New York *Post* is a convenient example) cast their plati-

tudes in phrases which give some indication of acquaintance
with psychoanalysis although they do not usually use many
technical terms. One Franzblau column replies to the parents
of a little boy with an I.Q. of 168. They were afraid that beginning first grade at four and a half in an "advanced school"
would speed the boy's intellectual development too far ahead
of his social maturity: he would be too small for games and,
later, too young for dates. The columnist reminded her cor-
respondents that a high I.Q. did not guarantee achievement
although it made achievement likely. Good schools, furthermore, dealt with gifted children more intelligently than merely
having them skip grades. The parents were really either fearful that the child would soon outstrip their authority or, worse
perhaps, pleased that he would fulfill their own frustrated
ambitions.

The child then comes to feel that his high marks are not for
himself, but as a gift or some kind of repayment to his parents.
When the youngster reaches the age of rebellion, he chooses this
vulnerable spot *to hit* back at the parents. [He fails to achieve.]
True he suffers somewhat, too, but he has the satisfaction of becoming the focus of the parents' concern and agitation.

The parents are thus confronted with threats to their narcissism or with the consequences of the child's revolt against
being exploited. They are made to feel somewhat guilty, then
reassured. The column concludes:

On the one hand, you are very thrilled about having a child
who is so unusual, but on the other hand you are perhaps over-
anxious and already worrying about the future. You are also fearful about making mistakes. Such over-anxiety inevitably transmits
itself to the child and frightens him, creating troubles instead of
pleasure.
    . . . Plan for today, rather than for a future ten years from now,
and your youngster will look forward to learning with pleasure
and gratification that brings real relaxation.[10]

10 New York *Post*, July 14, 1965, p. 39.

Presumably, parents given to anxiety can, after reading such counsel, purge themselves of their fears and rear their gifted child in non-neurotic attitudes toward living.

Another column presents the perennial conflict between mother and adolescent daughter. A sixteen-and-a-half-year-old describes herself as "quite cute" and wants to date an ex-steady of whom her mother disapproves "for certain reasons I don't care to mention." Forbidden to see the boy, the girl writes: "I feel my mother has no right to run my life."

The girl is told that she must be insecure, or she would not be so ready to make any invitation a command performance. Dr. Franzblau then proceeds to interpret mother to daughter, to point out:

> . . . Your mother is not running your life, but is only asking that you do not run helter-skelter back and forth, breaking and resuming a relationship that is no good for you. . . .
> When you have reached the emotional as well as the chronological age of self-support, then you will have the right to run your own life. Whether you run your life well or poorly then will depend on whether you listen to your parents' loving counsel now.[11]

The voice is the voice of Jacob still, although the vocabulary is somewhat altered: parental authority is upheld not in the name of religiously required obedience but in the name of promoting psychological maturity.

The very notion of remote-control psychological counseling runs contrary to the definition of psychotherapy as a direct encounter between persons. So long as such counseling limits itself to generalities, it can do little damage; indeed, it may help troubled persons to understand that it is not shameful to seek professional help. But the counseling columns and TV or radio programs do their harm on another level; they encourage readers to believe themselves informed when their ignorance has barely been disturbed. Problems are presented

[11] *Ibid.*, July 7, 1965, p. 31.

in abbreviated fashion with anything offensive to a general audience carefully removed. Condensation and censorship may be necessary, but they operate to distort the case itself. The counselor's evaluation can have no real depth; the counsel offered does not differ very much from what any reasonably sensible friend might give. Common sense proffered in "the paper" has an authority it might not have otherwise, of course. But such authority often is far too seriously regarded. People whose knowledge of psychology is limited to such columns tend to take the advice given there as the final word and proceed to apply their own interpretations of that word to the problems of their friends, their spouses, and their children.

The "quality" magazines discuss psychoanalysis and psychology on a higher level of popularization than the newspaper columns. Their articles are usually sober and well informed. Yet one wonders how much their readers actually profit from the information so imparted. Many people who have reasonably good educations continue to be disquietingly uncertain even about the goals and methods of psychoanalysis. After five decades, during at least four of which Freud and psychoanalysis have been rather generally talked about, it seems necessary to *The New York Times*, which has a presumably literate audience, to distinguish between psychiatry and psychoanalysis and to describe some of the actual procedures in analytic therapy.[12]

Since paperback books have large circulations, they, too, may be considered mass media, and they present a more complicated aspect of the popularization of Freud and psychoanalysis. Paperback publication has made Freud's own works —along with other psychoanalytic and psychological classics —available to anyone with a few dollars to spend. Moreover, the desire of publishers of paperbacks to have more and more books to sell has created a demand for books about psychoanalysis written for lay readers. The success of such books

[12] D. W. Wooley, "New Insight into Mental Illness," *Atlantic Monthly*, July, 1965, pp. 46–50, see also *The New York Times Magazine*, October 21, 1962.

reveals a general interest in psychoanalytic and psychological material. Sometimes, of course, the interest appears to center on sensation rather than true understanding: whatever its actual content, a book called *Deadly Reasons* is bound to draw readers interested in murder. Interest which actually centers on comprehension—and a good deal of it seems to do so—does indicate awareness of the need to understand people, an awareness which is encouraging in a time and a society which tend to prefer techniques to persons. Some of the paperback popularizations of Freud, like Eric Berne's book mentioned earlier, may have gaudy wrappings but do, nevertheless, convey a good deal of basic information.

Much current popularization is based on case histories. Some of these, Jean Evans' *Three Men*, for example, are straightforward presentations, interesting but not melodramatized. Other writers use themselves as case material and describe their own analyses. This sort of autobiographical presentation may be serious journalism like Lucy Freeman's *Fight against Fears*; it may be an anonymous work like *The Story of My Psychoanalysis*, currently out of print, which puts analytic treatment on the level of *I Was a Teenage Communist*; or it may, like Joyce McIver's *The Frog Pond*, be sensational fiction claiming to be based on the author's own experience with psychoanalysts.

Some case histories are the work of qualified experts who tell about patients they have helped—or even about those they have failed to help. Sometimes these may do more real harm than obvious sensationalism. Since these books are written by qualified professionals, they are taken seriously. Yet studies like those in Robert Lindner's *The Fifty-Minute Hour* and Harold Greenwald's *Great Cases in Psychoanalysis* do very little better than the more sensational books in the essential task of education: they present neither the dynamics of neurosis nor the basic principles of analytic treatment. Like the more sensational writers, the professionals' concern with maintaining style requires that material be condensed and accelerated in a way which must give the lay person a misleading picture of psy-

choanalytic therapy. If a reader of such books does seek treatment, his analyst may well have to spend a good deal of time
disabusing him of the notion that psychoanalysis is as simple
or as dramatic a procedure as that reported in fictionalized case
histories.

Further, a surprising number of readers identify with the
people described in dramatized case histories. Many girls, for
instance, identify with Robert Lindner's Laura in her over-
eating, oedipal involvement with her father, and even simulated
pregnancy.[13] Readers of case histories may interpret their own
behavior and that of people they encounter in the light of
what they have read. Such jumping to conclusions can provoke
real and unnecessary emotional distress, just as reading the
labels on patent medicine bottles once convinced people that
they had an assortment of physical diseases. And self-medica-
tion is ill-advised in psychotherapy even more than in other
fields. In one sense, of course, the patient in psychoanalysis
does heal himself. On the other hand, he needs more expert
guidance toward insight and the application of insight than he
can obtain by reading books that present the dramatic high-
lights of someone else's analysis. Only after a reasonably successful analysis can a person usefully apply what he has learned
to the analysis of his own feelings.

As we remarked earlier, the presence of numerous schools
of analytic thought in the United States has operated to make
laymen even more uncertain about what psychoanalysis actually is. Many of the neo-Freudian groups claim to have the
real key to analytic therapy; their brand alone is genuine, all
others mistaken or harmful. Some post-Freudian groups have
frankly abandoned basic Freudian concepts like the primary
importance of sexuality; others have shifted emphasis in therapy
from past history to current behavior. In the theory and practice of these new schools, classical analysis has been changed:
"corrected," the neo-Freudians say. Some of the change may
have been useful in giving a more sociological emphasis to

[13] Robert Lindner, *The Fifty-Minute Hour* (New York: Rinehart,
1955).

theories of human development, thus modifying some of the rigidity which has been charged against orthodox Freudians who are said to fail to approach the unique problems of people trying to live in our contemporary world. Some of the change, however, in its emphasis on the need for adjustment to the demands of the patient's social environment, has tended to reinforce de-individualizing trends in current social development. Psychotherapists who hold this adjustment approach to therapy may, as has been pointed out, even reinforce contemporary trends like the imposition of conformity.

The neo- and post-Freudian schools of therapy might well deny that they are oriented toward a "religious" approach to existence. Many members of these schools are deeply concerned with the issue of "values": of standards of behavior and of the role of the analyst in helping the patient whose standards are vacillating—or even, to all appearances, nonexistent—develop some concepts of what is worthwhile. Here the identity problem is especially relevant: the person who is uncertain about who and what he is may well be uncertain about what criteria he should use in appraising his conduct.[14]

Religion, of course, concerns itself with values, and Chapter 6 deals more fully with the curious alliance which has been concluded between psychoanalysis and a number of religious leaders. Politics is said to make strange bedfellows, but in this instance, the popularization of psychoanalysis has operated as an even stranger matchmaker.

Popularization and the Patient

Americans are said to be averse to strenuous intellectual effort, and despite all Freud's clarity and skill as a writer, an understanding appreciation of his thought requires such effort. The peculiarly American desire to receive information in predigested form is paralleled by a desire for quick remedies

[14] Allen Wheelis, *The Quest for Identity* (New York: Norton, 1958), p. 163.

to all problems, both personal and social. Where patience is
a virtue so little practiced, the demand that the way be made
easy has tended to distort attitudes toward analytic therapy
as well as to dilute understanding of analytic theory. In spite
of glib talk, there is an appalling ignorance about the dynamics
of analytic treatment. Notions about the effects of "being put
on the couch" have become so ingrained that contemporary
analysts find themselves obliged to spend time clearing away
accumulated misinformation in order that their patients may
gain some real understanding of the process of psychoanalysis.

American society moves so fast and the individual is carried
along so rapidly that analytic treatment often seems unreward-
ingly slow. Often patients are ill-prepared to invest the time,
money, and effort required by an analysis which may take two
to five years. For all the acceptance which psychoanalysis en-
joys, many people who need and want treatment are disturbed
by prevailing misconceptions. These errors have been little
affected—indeed they sometimes have even been increased—by
the role which counselors play in referring patients to psychotherapy. To repeat, many Americans have had their ideas about
analytic treatment shaped and distorted by popular books, by
the preaching of certain clergymen, and by the versions of
psychoanalysis shown in some films. Counselors of many types
—social workers, ministers, guidance personnel in schools,
clinical psychologists without analytic training—often do little
to dispel the ignorance of the people whom they advise. When
counselors refer clients for further treatment, they sometimes
do so with no further preparation than, "You need some
analysis or therapy," otherwise giving the client no clue as to
what psychotherapy actually is or how it differs from counseling itself. Consequently, the prospective patient—already
afflicted by problems or he would not be referred for additional help—is thrown unprepared into an entirely novel
situation.

In business, and even in ordinary social life, Americans are
accustomed to seek, and often to find, some quick resolution

of a problem. It is not hard to understand, therefore, why they find it difficult to accept the key premise of analytic treatment: no quick solution is to be had. The contemporary patient lives in a world where efficiency is worshipped, speed is prized, and "time is money." In analysis, however, there is no time to hurry. Frequently a patient whose mental picture of psychoanalysis has developed out of the simplistic dramatizations of the mass media is bored and disappointed with his analysis. Dependency is another frequent and troublesome problem—especially when a patient has moved from counseling to analytic psychotherapy. Americans are proverbially resistant to authority. Yet people with identity problems—and increasing numbers of patients give evidence of having such problems—tend to look for guidance outside themselves. The analyst who remains silent, as is often necessary, especially at the beginning of treatment, seems unsympathetic and unhelpful. Before genuinely analytic treatment can begin, therefore, the patient's desire for the analyst to use directive or supportive methods must be explored and dealt with as a form of resistance.

Actually, the most harmful distortion in popular treatments of Freudian thought and of psychoanalysis is a sin of omission: the absence of real effort to help readers understand that what happens in psychoanalysis is essentially a process of growth and that the potential for growth which analysis can offer the patient is far more important than its contribution to a solution of his current problems.

Yet the very idea of growth as a gradual process seems alien to the patient who thinks in terms of "cure." He is accustomed to the pace of life in a world which gives people little time to think, to pause, to evaluate. The patient is often entirely unprepared for the tempo of the analytic experience. Some of his lack of preparation springs from the misleading notions purveyed by popularizers. More of that lack, however, derives from the very character of American society, where the individual finds few chances and little encouragement to be spontaneously himself. Every phase of living, from earning a living to having sex, is so organized and scheduled that a man's life, it would seem, can proceed without his paying any genuine attention to it or feeling any real involvement in it. His sex life, for example, has become as "organized" as any other form of mass recreation.

We are not talking of prostitution, although this institution continues to exist and even to be employed as a means of selling other goods (at intervals one hears of the proffer of call girls to purchasing agents as an inducement to prefer the output of one supplier of industrial materials to that of another supplier offering the same steel beams, say, at an identical price). Rather we refer to aspects of the mores which organize the association of boys and girls and envelop that association in the atmosphere of a hothouse. Pairing off is encouraged even in rather young children (often under color of joke, of course). The ritual of dating is performed by people at increasingly younger ages. Eleven- and twelve-year-olds leaving the sixth grade for junior high school honor the occasion with proms and all the trappings of courtship. "Going steady" is an almost obligatory practice. In societies where marriages are not arranged by the older generation, young men and women have long had ways of meeting one another and improving the acquaintance. Yet the nineteenth-century male had more latitude than is allowed the male of our day, unless he is prepared to be considered queer; then he could avoid dating, if he chose, postpone marriage, or even not marry at all. Currently, it seems that an organizational society's pressures for conformity reinforce the high levels of the sex drive in late adolescence and the early adult years. Young people feel challenged to demonstrate their sexual capabilities while avoiding or minimizing genuine intimacy, "playing it cool," to use the colloquial term. Evading deep involvement with others lessens the risk of being hurt, and living in the shadow of possible destruction makes evasion seem sensible and acceptance of emotional risk quixotic. To this observer's eye, contemporary

American society seems to organize its members' sex lives in ways that lessen need for serious individual choice—it is dating or "making out" or being married that seems important, not sexual activity with some person who, for a time at least, engages one's being.

Oddly enough, perceptive sociologists like Whyte and Reisman feel able to study the relationship between society and the individual in the United States without paying much attention to the role of sex in the life of the contemporary American. It has been said that Freudian psychoanalysis destroyed Victorian taboos on sexuality in the United States. This is scarcely true. The taboos exist in many segments of the society. The modifications of psychoanalysis which have been so general in America frequently play down the role of sex in generating neurosis or shaping the personality. Even the remaining concern with sex is too much for an existential analyst like Thomas Szasz, who says "The Christian religion and [classical] psychoanalysis lend credence to a parochial obsession with sex."[15] Indeed, although a good segment of the middle class has become more permissive in their attitudes toward sexual behavior, sex has not ceased to be a problem. Freud thought the sex morality of his own time stood in need of sharp revision. He felt that unmitigated monogamy left much to be desired as a compromise between the demand for instinctual gratification and the demand for social order.[16] Once, restriction of sexuality had husbanded energy and channeled it for social purposes; now, by generating neurotic incapacity and neurotic suffering that restriction was exacting too high a price. Freud developed no prescriptions, however. He laid the foundation for our comprehension of the place of sex in human conduct, but the

[15] Thomas Szasz, "Legal and Moral Aspects of Homosexuality," in Judd Marmor, ed., *Sexual Inversion* (New York: Basic Books, Inc., 1965), p. 135.

[16] James Strachey, ed., *The Standard Edition of the Complete Works of Sigmund Freud*, vol. IX (London: Hogarth Press and the Institute of Psychoanalysis, 1953–).

dynamics of sexual behavior continue to require exploration because they shape, and are shaped by, life in today's organizational society.

The Soil and the Plant

It has been possible to popularize Freud in the United States because psychoanalysis had a unique contribution to make in a society where change is the rule. Many people living in this society have not known what was happening to their lives. Inherited non-rational allegiances—religious, philosophical, ideological—have lost much of their force. This loss of force —which has been proceeding at an increasing rate since the eighteenth century—has deprived many people of psychological support, as we said earlier. More and more such people have felt this loss and searched for support elsewhere.

Because such searching attitudes were present, it was possible to bring psychoanalysis to a lay audience in more serious (as well as sensational) fashion. Shakow and Rapaport in their 1964 monograph on the *Influence of Freud on American Psychology* point out that many young intellectuals accepted Freud without much genuine understanding because he seemed to support the rebelliousness of the 1920's. Freudian theory served to bolster the attack on Victorian rigidities, especially in respect to sex. Once victorious, however, the erstwhile rebels began to look for new certainties.

In a culture characterized by rapid social and technological change and experiencing a continuous displacement of old commands and old sanctions, personality patterns tend to be less stable than in cultures where change comes more slowly. When patterns are thus unstable, new ideas and new methods of dealing with personal problems are more necessary as well as more acceptable than in cultures where the impact of change is cushioned by time. Psychoanalysis, accordingly, has been more fully accepted here than it has been in Europe. Once criticized as a fad of rich women who needed only to be set to work over a washtub in order to be cured of their fancied illnesses, psychoanalysis has come to be treated as a road to self-understanding (or at least to the ready labeling of other people's behavior, and even one's own). Acceptance has been achieved, in part at least, through popularization. Freud has been read far less than have his expositors, and popularization has entailed distortion, at times; but it has also served to make more people willing to seek necessary therapy or to become aware that psychoanalysis can serve as a uniquely useful method for increasing understanding of their relationships to themselves and to external reality, including the other people who inhabit it. Unlike conventional methods by which people "place" themselves in existence, psychoanalysis offers a means of fitting oneself into the world without requiring that one submit to a new kind of institutional authority. Effective analysis, indeed, requires that irrational allegiances be understood and avoided; indeed, when such an allegiance arises in the patient-analyst relationship, it becomes an object of the analyst to analyze that situation so that the irrational element in the allegiance can be dissolved.

In the changing culture of America during the next decades individuals will continue to need the help that psychoanalysis can give. The continued popularization of certain analytic concepts may proceed on a higher level, increasing readers' willingness to read more and more carefully. Thus by furthering more thorough study of psychoanalytic ideas by educated persons, popularization may, in the long run, mitigate the effect of the distortions it will undoubtedly continue to generate.

4 · The Post- and Neo-Freudians

4 · The Post- and Neo-Freudians

Some thirty years ago, Freud wrote C. L. Oberndorf: "... the popularity of the term psychoanalysis in America is no evidence of a friendly attitude toward the subject or a particularly broad dissemination of, or profound understanding of its teachings." In one sense, Freud was right: he and his thought have become influential in America in ways he might not have approved. Certainly, he would have been keenly aware of the incongruity between America's cultural style and his own.

Generally speaking, American culture is optimistic and manipulative. History and nature both have been kind to the United States. Its physical environment is admirably suited to the requirements of a modern industrial economy. Its history has been free from the sociological and psychological pressures of a feudal past or the presence of powerful neighbors. Optimism is natural to a people with such an experience. To Americans no issues seem truly beyond human resolution, although it may often seem proper to evade issues. Once a problem is acknowledged, however, the American is apt to think it can be solved by spending enough money and energy. The context in which the problem has arisen may not be thoroughly investigated; the repercussions of attempts to deal with it may not be adequately considered—indeed, concern with context and repercussions may be dismissed as concentration on "mere theory."

Freud, on the other hand, is toughly rationalistic rather

than merely pragmatic. He is pessimistic in tone and at least ambivalent in his confidence regarding man's power to resolve his most important problems. Freud pursues human experience to its depths. Americans, on the other hand, even though their culture is rooted in a darkling Calvinism, generally prefer that men keep experience on the surface. American culture has been called antisexual; certainly it often treats its physical environment in ways that show it to be anti-sensuous. Hostility to sensuous enjoyment seems to express itself in positive delight in the ugly. Freud concerned himself with esthetics, not as an artist (although he was an artist in the use of language) but in his concern with the font of creativity from which art sprang; and for Freud, creativity too came from that sexuality and its permutations which were the fundamental element of human experience. Whether man's existence was viewed from the standpoint of the individual or of the group, it could be understood only in terms of the tensions arising from the need for gratifying the instinctual drives of sex and aggression and the need to restrain the expression of those drives in order that man might live in society. Life, Freud said, was hard to endure. Clearly, his methods and ideas had to be modified before psychoanalysis could be incorporated into American culture.

New Forms of Analytic Therapy

Had Freud lived into our time, he might have been no less critical about the changes which have occurred in psychoanalysis in America than he was disappointed in the quality of its early reception there. Traditional analytic treatment has been markedly altered. Often a classical analyst will see patients fewer than five times a week. Often the patient chooses to sit up and face his analyst rather than lie on the couch. Frequently, the analyst allows himself to appear as a person engaging in an active interchange with the patient rather than as a presence against which the patient bounces the ball of his memories, his phantasies, his distortions, and his clarifications.

There has been a significant increase in lay analysis in America, a practice which Freud, incidentally, strongly supported.[1] Moreover, the rise in the number of lay analysts is an outgrowth of the development of divergent schools of psychoanalytic thought, several of which maintain both training institutes for non-medical analysts and clinics where treatment is available.[2] Yet more important in increasing the number of lay analysts is the rising demand for psychotherapy as the stress of living in our time pushes people into a search for new kinds of help in solving their problems. Calls for assistance far outstrip the number of trained people available; hence a variety of shortcuts have come into use. Some concentrate on abbreviating therapy. Others, like group therapy in its many versions, try to use the supply of trained analysts to treat more people. Still others try to train more therapists, people who can give troubled individuals some help, recognize situations they are unable to handle, and make appropriate referrals.

Franz Alexander and his Chicago co-workers have experimented in shortening the treatment period while still applying psychoanalytic principles. Here, as in the case of the development of group therapy, we see how, under the pressure of demand for treatment, even European-trained analysts have sought to devise methods for "sharing the wealth." Although Alexander and his group have reported good results, analysts

---

[1] In July, 1938, Freud wrote: "I cannot imagine how that silly rumor of my having changed my views about the problem of Lay-Analysis may have originated. The fact is, I have never repudiated these views and I insist on them even more intensely than before, in the fact of the obvious American tendency to turn psycho-analysis into a mere housemaid of Psychiatry." Freud's attitude toward lay analysis is fully discussed in chapter 9 of Jones's third volume. (Ernest Jones, *The Life and Works of Sigmund Freud* [New York: Basic Books, Inc., 1957]).

[2] Among the clinics connected with the various neo-Freudian schools are those maintained by the William Alanson White Institute, which generally follows the ideas of Harry Stack Sullivan, and that associated with the American Institute of Psychoanalysis, which teaches and practices the version of psychotherapy Karen Horney developed.

who are firm in insisting that only classical technique can help the patient reconstruct his personality retain their original opinions; however useful other methods may be, they relieve symptoms but do not get to the roots of neurosis; hence they are not psychoanalysts.

Group therapy does not necessarily seek to cut the time a patient is in treatment but rather to extend the analyst's ability to serve and, further, to use group dynamics as a means of treatment. Freud might well have considered group therapy something of an absurdity, but its use reflects certain distinctly American problems, especially the loneliness which often brings people into group therapy as a way of learning to make themselves more acceptable to, and better able to cope with, other people. Patients in group therapy meet with an analyst in groups of eight or ten people of similar or varied background, of one sex or of both, of differing degrees of emotional disturbance (although therapists are very cautious in introducing borderline psychotics into a group). As problems are presented and talked about, patients and analyst seek to find the unconscious factors creating those problems and to develop methods of coping with them. Transference relations are formed among group members as well as with the therapist and by analyzing those relations and members' responses to what other members say (or don't say), patients learn to see themselves and their behavior more realistically. Again, the classical analyst might acknowledge that useful improvement may be gained from group therapy without admitting that this can be called psychoanalysis or, more important, that it can operate to change the personality in any fundamental way.

In an effort to equip more people to give analytic therapy, social service case workers, clergymen, doctors in general practice have been taught to give psychoanalytically oriented counseling. Teachers and school guidance workers have been drawn into the field.

Even more unconventional shortcuts have been employed. The value of the sympathetic listener has been recognized to the degree that the American army in Germany trained noncoms in the art of listening so that soldiers could "ventilate" their problems. This approach has been reported as having good results, at least in reducing the Army's rate of hospitalization for psychosomatic ailments. It has even been suggested that housewives be trained to do psychotherapy. Karen Horney saw a place for self-analysis—provided that the person seeking to treat himself was well educated and had had sufficient analytic treatment to see himself and his problems with the necessary clarity.[3] Group therapy is another method of extending the effectiveness of trained therapists, of training people in other professions—social workers and ministers, for example, to give more effective help to the people who bring problems to them—and of giving more people the benefit of treatment.

As Freud approved of lay analysis, so he would probably have accepted attempts to provide analytic therapy for a larger number of patients, Indeed, as early as 1918, he forecast a time when such facilities would become available.[4] But one wonders how Freud would have regarded the curious transformation which his theories and his attitudes have undergone in America. Freud, it has been said, was not a Freudian. Everyone knows that he was trained as a scientist, but he clearly did not intend to establish an orthodoxy, despite his

[3] See Morton M. Hunt and Rena Corman, *The Talking Cure* (New York: Harper and Row, 1965, pp. 19–22). Maya Pines, "Training Housewives as Psychotherapists" (*Harper's*, April, 1962) makes an interesting case though not one which convinces the professional. See also, Karen Horney, *Self-Analysis* (New York: Norton, 1942).

[4] "I will cast a glance," Freud said in 1918 to his colleagues at The Budapest Psychoanalytic Congress, "at a situation which belongs to the future—one that will seem fantastic to many of you, but which, I think nevertheless, deserves that we should be prepared for it. You know that the therapeutic effects we can achieve are very inconsiderable in number. . . . Now let us assume that by some kind of organization we are able to increase our numbers to an extent sufficient for treating large masses of people. . . . Then clinics and consultation departments will be built, to which analytically oriented physicians will be appointed." (Cited in C. P. Oberndorf, *A History of Psychoanalysis in the United States* [New York: Grune & Stratton, 1953], pp. 246–47.)

conviction that his approach alone constituted psychoanalysis. Indeed, he had himself developed those doctrines through a constant process of change, and he anticipated further changes in its basic doctrines. (It is worth noting that one of the most important developments in Freudian thought, the emphasis on ego-psychology, was initiated in large measure by Anna Freud, who certainly worked in her father's tradition.) It would be totally inaccurate to consider that Freud regarded himself as the formulator of some final truth which he had cast in an immutable form. Still, one is free to think that Freud might well have been displeased, and perhaps wryly amused, at some of the specific changes which occurred in psychoanalytic theory as psychoanalysis became acceptable in America. He would have remarked particularly on the dilution of his sexual theories, the softening of his deterministic and materialistic orientation, and the blurring of his tragic or, if you will, his pessimistic view of man.

Dissidence in the Twenties

After the years in which Freud was either unknown or castigated, American psychiatrists, psychologists, and psychotherapists began to develop approaches of their own. Clara Thompson maintains that the 1920's were the most crucial period in producing a definite reevaluation of Freudian psychoanalysis. She contends that Freud's theory during the twenties (when he was developing such concepts as the drive towards self-destruction and the psychic counterforces of Eros and Thanatos) had "remarkably little effect on its application to patients." To some psychotherapists in the twenties, it seemed evident that analytic treatment had failed with many of those they had tried to cure. At this time, too, Freud himself expressed strong doubts about the effectiveness of psychoanalysis in helping patients overcome their neurotic ailments, and in any event, psychoanalysis could be used only with a rather restricted range of patients; psychotics, particularly, were not amenable to analytic treatment.[5] Yet a large number of the trained psychiatrists in the United States were occupied with psychotic patients.

Care of the insane had been quite elaborately institutionalized in the United States. Most public institutions were within the range of state administrations, of course, and the care they provided varied widely. When such institutions were professionally staffed (and political influence sometimes operated to keep professionalism on a rather low level), those individual administrators were psychiatrists; hence concern with the severely disturbed and psychotic person tended to overshadow concern with the merely neurotic person, who could function in the general community however much of a problem he might be to himself and his family. Psychotherapy, which was not applicable to psychotic patients, seemed rather irrelevant to many psychiatrists. People like Harry Stack Sullivan—who had spent years at St. Elizabeth's, the Federal mental hospital, serving the residents of Washington, D.C.—may have recognized the validity of many of Freud's insights into the origin of emotional disturbances but they wanted to make those insights more useful in the treatment of psychotic patients.

In office practice, meanwhile, doctors and lay analysts alike found much in their experiences which suggested that neurosis was a disease of the total personality. Oskar Pfister—the Swiss clergyman who has been mentioned earlier as one of Freud's disciples, a man who maintained his allegiance to the end in spite of disagreement on the psychological nature of religious belief—anticipated the concept of psychotherapy which some neo- and post-Freudians were going to develop. Pfister's ideas seem to foreshadow one of the characteristic aspects of psychoanalysis in the United States: its role as a means of helping people accept their existence rather than a method of treating only marked emotional disturbance. As he wrote Freud in 1926, an "enormous number of adults" were not "ill in the

[5] Clara Thompson, *Psychoanalysis: Evolution and Development* (New York: Grove Press, 1957).

medical sense but nevertheless in extreme need of analysis," and Pfister cited as instances "alcoholics, people with warped lives, those whose love life has gone astray, frustrated artists, etc."[6]

Encounters with patients with similar problems convinced Trigant Burrow that effective psychoanalysis must treat the entire personality and that the entire personality could be understood only against the social background in which that personality had developed. This conclusion served as the basis for Burrow's own later work in developing group therapy. Burrow's experience in that field confirmed him in the opinion that patients' distortions of reality duplicated attitudes which appeared in socially acceptable forms in persons who were considered normal. The social norms, Burrow argued, were themselves at fault because they operated to focus attention on the behaviorally isolated self and not on the species. Since organisms and environment interact through attention, failure to focus attention properly accounted for both social problems and individual neurosis. Burrow shifted his own focus accordingly, and for three decades after 1917 pursued group studies on the way in which the contemporary human organism diverted its attention from the wholeness of its relation to the environment and concentrated instead on its own separated special feelings, a concentration which could be located in the physical nervous system.[7]

Burrow reports Freud as having exclaimed to a mutual friend: "Does Burrow think he is going to cure the world?" and himself as replying: "I most certainly do."[8] He left psychoanalysis behind in the effort and turned to very specialized physiological research.

Other analysts did not go so far. Many even failed to draw upon the more conventionally analytic aspects of what Burrow

---

[6] Heinrich Meng and Ernst Freud, *Sigmund Freud: Psychoanalysis and Faith* (New York: Basic Books, Inc., 1963), p. 104.

[7] Trigant Burrow, *Science and Man's Behavior* (New York: Philosophical Library, 1963), pp. 24–28; 182–203.

[8] *Ibid.*, p. 120.

had done. They, too, however, moved from the classical analytic procedure of considering the patient as an isolated individual to a new orientation which led them to regard the patient as a person who had to live in relationship with others and who suffered when neurotic attitudes distorted his efforts to relate. Thus, some of Freud's followers moved from a view of the patient as a self-contained being to seeing him in interaction with the society in which he functioned. This shift induced such analysts to scrutinize and even to criticize society itself. Before examining the views of those who have developed the post- and neo-Freudian approaches to psychoanalysis, it is worthwhile to look at a few significant points of divergence between Freud and those who have moved away from, or (if one prefers) beyond him.

An initial distinction should be made between the post- and neo-Freudians who hold him in high regard and accept much of what he thought and taught, and the followers of Jung and Adler who, by and large, reject or very seriously modify aspects of psychoanalysis, such as the role of unconscious factors in neurotic behavior. Jung, of course, accepted the unconscious but treated it as mystic might. Adler's disciples tend to concentrate on present problems and to center their thinking around power: the child's experience of helplessness and inferiority to adults operates to shape his future style of life.

Jung and Adler both set aside the Freudian stress on infantile sexuality. This is not true of all post- and neo-Freudian thinking, although often disturbances of sexual development are not the center of attention in therapy, and sexuality is redefined until it bears less resemblance to an instinctual drive than to a pattern of interpersonal relations. The Oedipus complex, for example, is seen in terms of desire to be possessively dependent on another person rather than in terms of a wish for sexual possession of the parent of the opposite sex, and thus becomes an aspect of interpersonal relations rather than of psychosexual development. One might see this change in Freudian terms as a symptom of a return to repression: deepseated hostility to sexuality, apparently submerged in permissiveness, nevertheless emerges, operating to make problems of sexuality only secondary factors in generating neurosis. Even analysts trained in Europe appear reluctant, when they undertake practice in America, to equate their acceptance of the theory of sexuality with their psychoanalytic approach. It seems that even in the mid-twentieth century, Freud's emphasis on sexuality as the primary factor molding human personality is more than many people, even psychoanalysts, can assimilate without psychological pain.

The neo-Freudians also reject much of Freud's libido theory with its biological determinism and unqualified materialism.[9] It is clear that, in interpreting patients' problems, neo-Freudian therapists regard consideration of his current environment, familial and social, as more helpful than the study of the tug of war between Eros and Thanatos—the desire to love and be loved and the desire to destroy and to die—which Freud postulates as going on in the individual. Again, because the neo-Freudians are concerned with the interaction between the patient and his past and present social environment, they are less interested in his infantile experience and its recrudescence in adult behavior.[10] As might be expected, therefore, the neo-Freudians have tended to replace what could be called an id-centered psychology with what might be called an ego-centered psychology: in their theory, the instinct-governed id loses ground before the more pragmatic ego. In the United States, Heinz Hartmann and Erik Erikson (who depart from Freud only in emphasis) are the best-known exponents of ego psychology, and it is interesting that Erikson, like Erich Fromm, came to psychoanalysis with a background in the social disciplines (sociology, in his case).

Listing the points of disagreement between Freud and his American successors in this way makes it seem, perhaps, that

[9] Martin Birnbach, *Neo-Freudian Social Philosophy* (Stanford, Calif.: Stanford University Press, 1961), p. 68.
[10] Karen Horney, *New Ways in Psychoanalysis* (New York: Norton, 1939), p. 153.

basic Freudian principles have been wholly rejected. This would not be true, however, even of Sullivan who probably went furthest in reinterpretation and in casting aside Freud's vocabulary and patterns of thought. For Sullivan, emotional disturbance was a disturbance in the relationship with "the others," whether parents, mates, friends, associates, or superiors. The therapeutic situation enabled the patient to examine his interpersonal relations through examination of his relationship with his analyst. Unlike the strict Freudians, Sullivan and his followers did not regard the analyst-patient relationship as a mere transference situation reproducing other, older relationships, but rather as a realistic experience in present time, an experience from which the patient could learn how to relate to other people. Hence Sullivan's followers encourage active interchange between patient and therapist although they do not go as far as Sandor Ferençzi[11] recommended in his contention that, as neurosis was the outcome of the failure to receive sufficient love from the parent, the therapist had to have a warm as well as an active relationship with the patient.

Karen Horney, herself a leader in neo-Freudian thinking, did not want to cut the intellectual bond between Freud and his heirs. Neo-Freudians, she wrote, accepted his views on the significance of "the unconscious forces" and the value of free association. Dreams were meaningful; the patient-analyst relation was important in therapy; the therapist must recognize and deal with the patient's defenses and his resistance in therapy. Thus, she concluded, there was a "common heritage which forms the groundwork of psychoanalytic theory and method."[12]

A neo-Freudian analyst, consequently, may deal with a

[11] Sandor Ferençzi (1873–1933) will be remembered as perhaps the most gifted of Freud's early followers and co-workers. Ferençzi's work on anality, aggression, and the pursuit of wealth is a particularly interesting contribution to analytic theory. Toward the end of Ferençzi's life, he and Freud broke on the issue of Ferençzi's alterations in classical therapeutic technique.

[12] Karen Horney, "Tenth Anniversary," *American Journal of Psychoanalysis*, XI, 1951.

patient in a manner resembling that used by a classical analyst, but he does so in a somewhat different spirit. He holds that neurotic behavior is not a series of isolated occurrences within the life history of a given individual. Rather such behavior is part of his total personality. To cite Horney again: ". . . every neurosis, no matter what the symptomatic picture, is a character neurosis." But this neurosis occurs because it seems to be the necessary although unsatisfactory adjustment to a society whose demands, when they become too heavy for a neurotic character structure, precipitate overt anti-social activity or press to the breaking point what is already a fragile instrument.[13]

Many neo-Freudians are deeply concerned with what they see as a connection between the society and the character of individual psychotherapy. Both institutions and the individual in America have been and are subjected to a greater degree of instability than they were half a century ago. Most neo-Freudians have been struck by this phenomenon, whether they are native to the American scene or view it with the fresher and perhaps more impartial eye of the foreigner. Sullivan saw neurosis in the patients he encountered as the outgrowth of insecurity and anxiety. Karen Horney found competitiveness to be the root from which anxiety and insecurity grew. Franz Alexander regarded competition itself as a consequence of the individual's effort to validate and establish a sense of his own uniqueness and integrity in an egalitarian society of conflicting values. Kardiner pointed out that contemporary society was the consequence of its past, that its egalitarian and competitive trends and pressures represented a long-term evolution of social institutions.[14] Those trends and pressures,

[13] Horney, *New Ways in Psychoanalysis*, p. 183.
[14] Abram Kardiner was among the first to present an analysis of the individual in Western society in terms of the historical evolution of Western, and other, social institutions and thus to give neo-Freudian thinking its most useful perspective for understanding the genesis and persistence of psychic disfunctioning in contemporary American society. (See *The Psychological Frontiers of Society*, New York: Columbia University Press, 1963, reprint.)

Erich Fromm argues, have combined to form "the marketing orientation" toward life, and living according to that orientation depletes the person by making his relations with others shallow and essentially unrewarding.

Psychotherapy and Society

Thus, the neo-Freudians have tended to link psychoanalytic theory and therapy with the character of the society in which the neurotic patient lives. In their view, mental illness and individual instability are generated by the very nature of modern Western society. The United States is the Western culture in which the development of a technological and industrial orientation to life has met no effective countervailing force—the United States has no feudal past, no recognized hereditary aristocracy, no militaristic tradition (however aggressive the nation may once have been), and no established church (however powerful the churches). Money alone has a prescriptive right to respect; and the possessors of money are more important as possessors than as persons. In America, then, only a threat to anticipated profit can stand in the way of the application of technology. The larger social consequences of such application are rarely regarded. When technological convenience seems to stand in conflict with a humanly tolerable environment (as in the destruction of natural beauty by the installation of overhead power lines), technology takes priority. Given their kind of value situation, it might well have been expected that the impact of mobility would produce both social and psychological instability in the United States, and that is, indeed, the case.

During the 1930's and 1940's, Sullivan and Horney were considered the most important exponents of new methods in psychotherapy and new concepts about neurosis. Sullivan's influence was exercised most directly upon those who studied with him; he was a rather clumsy writer and is less familiar to the general public than either Horney or Fromm. As has been mentioned, Sullivan stressed warping of interpersonal relations as the key factor in neurosis. In the psychotherapeutic relationship, he contended, the patient, who has not learned how to deal adequately with other people, gains a fresh opportunity to master a skill that he has failed to acquire. Although Sullivan thought character was shaped in the course of contact with "significant others," those "others" were seen as individuals rather than as elements in the society as a whole.

Karen Horney concerned herself with a larger social context than Sullivan. In her view, "the neurotic personality of our time" was created by the character of the time itself as well as by the individual's experience with other individuals. It is noteworthy that she, like Erich Fromm, should be a European, and one who had seen at first hand how defeat, inflation, and depression in Central Europe created a psychopathological orientation in a sufficient number of persons to make it possible for political leadership to promote a kind of collective madness.

Erich Fromm's discussion of the interaction between the character of the society and the neurosis of the individual has been widely read in the United States. He began his studies in that field in the late twenties and early thirties, but they have been best known to Americans since the Second World War. Some of the influence Fromm presently exerts is owing to his approach, which ranges far beyond the walls of the therapist's consulting room. Having started out as a sociologist, he came to psychoanalysis with a vision of man as a being shaped by a context far broader than that of oedipal rivalry in the family or even of the Freudian trinity—id, ego, and superego—as that develops within a given family constellation.

Fromm: Society and Neurosis

In both early works, like *Escape from Freedom*, and later studies, like *May Man Prevail?* Fromm has been concerned with man as a creature potentially free and morally obligated to protect and extend his freedom. Whether his subject involves the enslavement of men to authority or the conflict between the United States and Russia, it is obvious that he is dealing with the same phenomena. In Fromm's literary clinic, society is the patient. Like Rousseau, he believes that man is a victim of vicious institutions. Thus he has, in a sense, taken up where Freud left off, pushing on with research into the psychopathology of civilized communities. Like Trigant Burrow, Fromm believes that societies can be sick, but where Burrow searched for a neurobiological basis for cure, Fromm directed attention toward the society. Freud sought to replace id with ego, to make the unconscious conscious in the patient's personal life. Fromm attempts to persuade society to deal with itself as if it were a patient, to be more aware of its unexpressed major premises and, further, to be willing to try to change them when they are shown not to correspond to the reality of human needs. Fromm is more than social critic, then; he is also something of a social reformer, not in the sense of espousing specific causes, but rather in the sense of making continuous effort to persuade more and more people to see that they need to work to change the world in which they live and move and have their neuroses.

In this we see the chief difference between Fromm's revision of Freudian theory and that of other Freudian critics and remolders of psychoanalytic theory. Fromm, with his concern for man as a human being, rather than man as a patient, goes beyond psychoanalysis. Hence he is properly regarded as a post-Freudian rather than a neo-Freudian. He is less concerned with making psychoanalysis more adequate, therapeutically and theoretically, than he is with using psychoanalytic insights as a means of understanding contemporary man's plight and of controlling and directing the fate of man in our time.

Specifically, Fromm is interested in the situation of man in modern, urban, industrial society. In *The Sane Society*, he maintains that men, whether they live under communism or capitalism, will become more machinelike, more alienated from themselves and from others. They will be well fed, well clothed, well cared-for

> ... automatons, who follow without force, who are guided without leaders, who make machines which act like men and produce men who act like machines. . . . This alienation and automatization leads to an ever-increasing insanity. Life has no meaning, there is no joy, no faith, no reality. Everybody is 'happy'—except that he does not feel, does not reason, does not love. In the nineteenth century the problem was that "God is dead"; in the twentieth century the problem is that *man is dead*.[15]

Implicit in that statement is one of Fromm's important theoretical contributions to sociological and psychological thinking: the concept of *social character*, which he first presented in 1932.[16] Individual character, Freud had concluded, was to be understood in terms of libido; the character traits of individuals represented the differing ways in which they had developed sublimations of, or reaction formations against, the multiform aspects of the sexual drive. Fromm goes beyond the concept of character structure as a merely individual phenomenon. He maintains that nations and societies have a *social* character, and he defines it as ". . . the nucleus of the character structure which is shared by most members of the same culture." Within any given society, individuals will, of course, differ from one another and some of them will not fit the character structure of the society. They may be the deviants—delinquents or prophets—but even their deviation will tend to appear in forms that reflect socially generated patterns of attitude, action, and emotion.

Fromm contends, too, that social character shows how a particular society channels its energy. Most of the people in

---

[15] Erich Fromm, *The Sane Society* (New York: Rinehart, 1950), pp. 359–60.

[16] Fromm, *Beyond the Chains of Illusion* (New York: Simon and Schuster, 1962), p. 78. Also see his classic, as yet untranslated essay, "Die psychoanalytische Charackterologie und ihre Bedeutung für die Soziologie," *Zeitschrift für Sozialforschung* (1932).

that society will have similar motivations; they will share the same ideals and exert their effort in the same direction. Thus, social character is the "intermediary between the socio-economic structure and the ideas and ideals prevalent in the society.[17] Again, Fromm's deepest concern is with contemporary Western culture, the kind of industrial economy which the United States represents in its "purest" form, least diluted by survivals from a feudal past. Fromm thinks it has produced a kind of social character very different from that which prevailed in the nineteenth century, when the middle-class man stood in what ". . . in many ways can be called the 'hoarding situation.' Abstention from consumption, saving, and respect for authority were not only virtues, but they were also satisfactions for the average member of the middle classes; his character structure made him like to do what, for the purposes of his economic system, he had to do."[18] In contemporary society, however, the emphasis is not placed on saving and hoarding, but on consuming. Thus, as Fromm points out, current social character has one single aim: *using* —whereas the aim of the nineteenth-century social character was *having*. Emphasis on the economic aspects of social character is apparent throughout Fromm's work.

Fromm has also developed a scheme of character types which is an interesting example of the post-Freudian approach to classifying characters. He divides character into the productive and the non-productive and lists four types of the non-productive (1) receptive (accepting) masochistic, (2) exploitative (taking) sadistic, (3) hoarding (preserving) destructive, (4) marketing (exchanging) conforming.

In contrast to the working and loving person—the character type that results from a productive orientation[19]—the four character types just listed are all negative. Marketing man, of course, is the man of our day. He has no true identity; he is manipulator and manipulated. He thinks only in terms of

[17] Fromm, *Beyond the Chains of Illusion*, p. 87.
[18] *Ibid.*, p. 80.
[19] Fromm, *Man for Himself* (New York: Rinehart, 1947), p. 111.

commodities. According to him, the only thing worth considering is what a man brings into the market. His personal relationships are superficial and shallow in a way which has produced a great deal of the loneliness experienced by contemporary man. Because that loneliness is the outgrowth of the marketing orientation of the personality, it is "an illusion to expect that the loneliness of man rooted in the marketing orientation can be cured by individual love."[20]

What does Fromm see for the future? He hopes for the emergence of a new man who will operate in terms of the productive orientation toward life. Such a person will experience himself as "the embodiment of his powers" feeling one with them, yet aware of them. In many ways, Fromm's productive character resembles Freud's genital man, the person capable of love and of work. The productive character, too, has this capacity. He recognizes, moreover, that, as Fromm puts it, "the inner life must always be a life of conflict. This conflict, however, can be tempered by self-knowledge and curbed by reason. It can be lived with."[21]

Fromm is a social critic in the tradition of the Freud who wrote *Future of an Illusion* and *Civilization and its Discontents*. But Fromm does more than employ psychoanalytic concepts to show how understanding individual neuroses helps us understand religion and politics. Fromm goes beyond critics of classical psychoanalytic theory and technique; he has proceeded toward a sociological appraisal of psychoanalysts and their discipline. For years, he notes in *May Man Prevail?*, large numbers of analysts reflected the attitudes of the social group into which most of them were born and "tended to consider as neurotic anyone who deviated from this attitude, either to the left or to the right. Very few psychoanalysts had any serious political, philosophical, or religious interests beyond those customary in the urban middle class."

In contrast, Fromm himself was a social reformer. Freudian psychoanalysis had already exercised an important influence on twentieth-century America, he acknowledged; and American society needed the stimulation Freudian theory had brought into its intellectual life. But, he argued, if the encounter between Freud and America was to develop all its potentialities, more than Freudian clinical theory needed to be modified. Patients in a society like that of the contemporary United States had, of course, to be understood in terms of the culture which surrounded them. More than that, patients—and analysts —needed to be aware of the defects of their culture in order to modify it in desirable ways. Nor could desire to modify the culture be taken for a merely neurotic phenomenon; a means of escaping one's own problems by devoting oneself to those which afflicted the community. Other analysts besides Fromm, of course, have been aware of the relationship between trends in social development and shifts in psychoanalytic thought. Martin Birnbach, in particular, has shown how, in the discussion of social problems, analysts have made mental health "a significant value, perhaps the supreme value," both for individual life and for the evaluation of social institutions.[22] But Fromm has had both foresight and insight: he sensed that certain changes in social pattern were occurring, and he has consistently examined psychoanalytic theories about man's nature in the light of those changes.

The Contemporary Analyst

All post- and neo-Freudian modifications of psychoanalysis must be considered in terms of the experience of Americans and their society during the last three decades. The period has been characterized by affluence and an advancing technology; wealth has grown and income, at least, has been somewhat more evenly distributed in spite of poverty among the aged and the unskilled young. In this context of comfort, nevertheless, many have been aware of the decline in the role

[22] Birnbach, *op. cit.*, p. 210.

of the person *as* person in the process of sharing and experiencing life in its totality. The depersonalization, even the dehumanization of the individual, has been acutely felt and has in turn made it increasingly necessary that psychoanalysis reevaluate both itself and contemporary man in order to be effective as therapy and relevant as theory.

The "revisionists" (to use Eric Berne's term) retain the essential elements of Freudian therapy: they encourage free association; they interpret dreams; they explore the patient's past to see whether and how it is affecting present behavior. But they rank instinct as less important in generating neurosis than specific experience. They see that experience sharply affected by the social context in which a family leads its life. Partly because of their own experience in American life, they are keenly aware of the way in which change affects that context itself. Thus, their concern moves outward from the patient and back again.

Man and society are less fixed, less an unalterable "given" in the "revisionist" view than in that accepted by classical analysis. Consider their respective treatment of the Oedipus complex, for example. Orthodox Freudians see the male character as defined by the boy's innate sexual rivalry with the father, his hatred, his inevitable guilt, and hopefully, his final reconciliation: he recognizes reality, renounces possession of his mother and accepts his rival as model of maleness. If the process fails to move smoothly from stage to stage, the boy develops a form of neurotic disturbance closely associated with the stage where the failure occurred.

Some neo-Freudians assign the Oedipus complex only a minor place in creating neurosis. Others, sensitive to the role of the mother in the contemporary American family, admit the importance of the Oedipus complex but tend to describe it less in terms of rivalry between father and son than in terms of unwholesome intimacy (one might almost call it conspiracy) between son and a mother who, by ruling the house, diminishes the effectiveness of the father as an image of masculinity with which the boy can identify. Still others concentrate on the way in which social change has operated to make the mother so dominant a figure in the middle-class family as to distort the classic pattern of oedipal development. Very few, of course, have gone on to speculate whether the traditional family is a psychologically viable institution in the contemporary social context or whether traditional role expectations can be maintained without unforeseen social change on the one hand or an unprofitable degree of injury to mental health on the other.

The revisionists recognize Freud's continued influence in shaping the role of psychoanalysis in American society, but they also see a need for modifying analytic theory to emphasize those elements in it which are pertinent for the American individual today. The contemporary person seems to be more completely enmeshed in the society or organization in which he functions than was his nineteenth-century counterpart; his experiences and responsibilities and, consequently, his emotional problems are very different from those of people in nineteenth-century Vienna. Recognition of such difference in experience as a result of social change offers an important clue to the emergence and the character of psychoanalytic revisionism. Significantly, although Fromm first published his ideas about social and individual character and social and individual neurosis during the interwar period in Germany, they did not have their full impact on the United States until after the Second World War, when the structure of American society and the problems of people in that society made his ideas more readily acceptable.

Study of the character structure generated by the society has given the function of the psychoanalyst a new meaning. Again, this has occurred not merely in contradiction of Freudian theory but as a result of the contemporary disintegration of values. This disintegration, moreover, is a consequence of social developments, especially in the United States. The psychoanalyst often turns social philosopher insofar as he goes beyond the clinical aspects of the case and tries to fit it into the current content of society. As Erich Fromm puts it: "The psychoanalyst must study the personality and character structure of those who profess certain thought systems, both as individuals and as groups. He will inquire into the consistencies of character structure with professed opinion and will interpret the thought system in terms of the unconscious forces which can be inferred from minute details of manifest behavior."[23]

This procedure, Fromm declares, follows the essential points of Freud's characterology: that behavior allows us to infer the character traits which lie beneath it, that those traits may be unconscious, and that they are not to be viewed as discrete entities but as part of a whole which may be termed an "orientation of character."[24]

The concept of character orientation is perhaps the most important single contribution of the neo-Freudian movement to the development of analytic theory and to the growth of general acceptance of psychoanalysis in the United States. The concept is serviceable to the therapist who must so often, even in the purely clinical setting, act as social interpreter. The concept furthers the effort of therapist and social scientist to increase their understanding of the interaction between the individual and his culture, between the psychoanalytic and the sociological approach to human problems. As Birnbach points out, the neo-Freudian critique of psychoanalysis has tended to center researchers' attention on the larger social setting, the "pathological" situation which helps generate and tends to define the individual's pathology.

It may seem inconsistent at this point to note that, despite long and often embittered controversy between orthodox Freudians and neo-Freudians, there is surprisingly little difference in the way they handle patients. Or rather, there is surprisingly little discussion of the changing role of the ana-

[23] Fromm, *Man for Himself*, p. 57.
[24] Fromm, *The Sane Society*, p. 174.

lyst or of the patient, for that matter—although we hear much about the altered pattern of symptoms with which patients come to therapy.

The analyst encounters in his present-day American patients problems very different from those common in Freud's Vienna. Usually his patients were suffering from conflicts between internalized social expectations and social requirements (the superego) and unrecognized (i.e., suppressed) instinctual needs. Modern patients experience more subtle and far-reaching kinds of conflict. Partly as an outcome of the acceptance of Freud's ideas, instinctual needs are more generally recognized as natural and less a source of guilt and suffering than they once were. In our other-directed society, people experience different but equally distorting pressures. Disintegration of the family, greater personal and class mobility, the acceleration of change on every level, offer individuals in America far less supportive a setting than that to be found in the relative stability of Freud's society.

Today's American neurotic suffers from alienation and anxiety as he experiences a kind of identity crisis which would have been unimaginable to Europeans during the early years of this century. Consequently, in present-day psychotherapy the patient often requests counsel from the therapist and makes demands upon him which, if complied with, would cast the analyst in a role far different from that which classical Freudians assume. In regard to the transference relationship particularly, I believe that real (although gradual) change will occur as psychoanalysis gains even further ground and psychotherapy becomes a recognized tool for furthering not only the "adjustment" but the rebirth of the individual.

Freudian and neo-Freudian analysts alike have tended to serve as mirrors reflecting the patient's phantasies, to be father, mother, sibling, lover by turns, to exist for the patient not as real human persons but as a kind of effigy to be animated by the patient's own projected emotions. The analyst has confined himself to interpreting the situation, pointing out what the patient was doing in the analytic relationship and perhaps helping him to see how he has acted in similar ways outside the analytic situation. Generally, however, even the neo-Freudian analyst has not gone beyond that; he has not proceeded to undertake the further clarification of the changing role of the parties to the analytic transaction; yet such clarification is needed if the patient-therapist relationship is to be understood in the most fruitful way.

Today's analyst must become less the mere aloof clinician and more the "social interpreter." He must mediate between the anxious patient whose conflicts derive from his lack of a secure identity, and the social world which has made it so difficult for the patient to build an identity for himself. He must, in short, make patient and world known to one another. The analyst is not to impart his own values to the patient. The analyst as analyst is not obligated to become involved in larger social issues in the sense of affiliating himself with programs for reform. He must however be aware of the elements in contemporary society that generate problems for his patients; and in order to make that awareness effective and keep it keen, he must keep in contact with the trends in current social and philosophical thought which seek to understand the shifting conditions of human existence.

The revisionists have already made some contributions to help the analyst to become a more effective social interpreter. Fromm has written about the "illnesses" inherent in both the structure and the basic premises of a competitive society. Kardiner takes note of the dehumanization and the sense of depersonalization which affect so many patients when he writes that our society may become one in "which we live alone together, among but not with one another," and in so writing illuminates the contemporary therapeutic situation.

The sensation of being alone and insignificant contributes to the alienation which many Americans experience whether they are patients in psychotherapy or people who consider themselves in no special need of treatment. Indeed, Fromm believes that the concept of alienation should serve as a point of departure for today's analyst whether he is seeking to understand the character structure of a patient or contemporary social character in general.[25] Many people feel like impoverished objects, dependent on powers outside themselves onto which they have, Fromm says, projected their living substance.

In one way or another, many patients experience depleting feelings of nothingness. Outward experience seems insignificant; only inward experience counts, but the individual cannot be sure he is experiencing as an individual or, in fact, is experiencing at all.

For people who find themselves moving in life in this fashion, existentialism has a peculiar appeal both as a philosophy and as a method in psychotherapy. That appeal is reinforced by popularizations of existential thought which stress the willfulness and the rebellion against bondage to causation that can be found in existentialism. The main reasons for the popularity of existential thought resemble the reasons for the influence of Freud and his successors: on many levels ranging from the crude to the subtly philosophical, Americans confronted by the problems of living in our complicated, changing, and threatening society are seeking help. They are concerned with life, death, and existence in a world where traditional solutions carry increasingly little force (despite the current "return to religion") and where no one need do more than be present in order to live dangerously.

Freud and His Successors: the Fruits of Conflict

In this chapter, we have been concerned with two questions: What has been the influence of Freudian revisionism on psychoanalysis in the United States? Is that influence an extension of the general impact which Freudian theory has had in America? It seems clear that Freud's successors have profited

[25] Fromm, *Psychoanalysis and Religion* (New Haven: Yale University Press, 1950), p. 63.

by the initial impact of psychoanalysis in America and the subsequent need for their modifications of its theories. It seems clear, too, that the changes they have introduced tend to make psychoanalysis more acceptable to Americans; the tone as much as the content of many of the revisionists' ideas reflects the influence of the American temperament on analysis itself.

The reasons for the growing influence of all types of psycho-analytic therapy and theory are to be found in the emotional needs of the individual who lives in a mobile and demand-ing technological society. Those needs seem all the more urgent because at present there appears to be no serviceable, stabilizing image of man in general or of the person himself. Indeed, no such image has existed for a long time. Life in the post-Darwinian world has destroyed it. An increasing number of people have become aware that the image is broken. Yet that image is necessary in order that the individual may enjoy a sense of continuity within his own life and a feeling of being at home in the community where he functions. If such an image is not available to him, he finds it difficult to establish an inner certainty that in some undefined way, under any circumstance he may encounter, he will be himself, the same tomorrow as he was yesterday. To recognize the need for continuity is not to deny that change occurs within the person as well as outside him. But for that change to proceed without causing too much emotional strain, the person must have a reasonably constant image (and one reasonably correspondent to reality) of himself and of other people.

A man must internalize enough of his culture—social, ma-terial, psychological, religious—to give him a sense of being most "man" when he is most an individual. This sense of being man and individual simultaneously is part of the experience of becoming a civilized adult. The course of Western history has been such that it is difficult to conceive of a civilized person's being nothing more than a set of psychological dy-namisms functioning with minimal friction within a social group. He must be an individual. Yet he must also be part of a social group whose imperatives become part of himself. Such internalization of the culture gives a person the peg, as it were, on which to hang the garment of his feelings about himself and about those who are instrumental in making him significant during his lifetime. When this peg is inadequate in itself, when it is, furthermore, not solidly integrated into the personality, the individual lacks the psychological support necessary for his existence. Such people have failed to make certain needful identifications; this failure results in anxiety about the self within and in uncertainty about their role in the world.

When enough people are thus anxious and uncertain—and somehow aware of that anxiety—they become receptive to the idea of a thoroughgoing examination of themselves and even of their society. Readiness for self-examination makes people more open to new trends of thought which may further that examination and help increase and improve understanding. Under conditions like those experienced today, such a relatively critical approach to self and society comes to seem necessary to increasing numbers of people; in societies that still give people serviceable support in establishing stable images of man and of themselves, such self-understanding through self-scrutiny is impossible because it seems irrelevant, or even improper and dangerous.

The Freudian revisionists—with their emphasis on the social setting in which personal psychological problems arise, their relative willingness to find fault with that setting, their subordination of instinct to experience as a factor shaping the human personality, even their interpretation of sexuality in terms of interpersonal relations rather than mere biological drive—have seemed more relevant to many contemporary Americans than have the classicists even when those who consider themselves directly in line with classical analytic thought turn their attention to ego psychology. On the other hand, it has been asserted that the neo- and post-Freudian movement has added nothing but errors to Freud; in particular, it is contended that the innovators have not made one really significant new contribution to a reevaluation of the role of psychoanalytic thought in American society. This hardly seems a fair estimate when one considers the contributions of Franz Alexander, Erich Fromm, and Karen Horney. However, the work of the Freudian revisionists constitutes only part of the thinking which needs to be done about the psychological and sociological situation of contemporary America if Americans are to achieve, in psychotherapy or outside, the kind of understanding of themselves and their world that will help them to live as less anxiety-ridden persons. By blending interpretation of society with Freud's thinking about the psychological development of the individual, the post- and neo-Freudians have already made a useful contribution in broadening Freud's approach both clinically and, to use his term, "metapsychologically."

5 · Freud and Education

5 · Freud and Education

IN surveying the impact of Freud and Freudian thinking upon education in the United States, it is necessary to distinguish the contribution of Freudian thought to our understanding of the development of the human personality from the effect that a superficial acquaintance with Freudian theory has had upon the methods and objectives of formal school instruction. Failure to make this rather obvious distinction helps account for a number of current misunderstandings about and in American education. The outside observer, especially the observer educated in Europe, may well conclude that some professional educators in America have become so ready to apply Freudian insights that they have forgotten the difference between rearing a child in the home and teaching a child in school.

Whatever reservations one may have, it is certain that understanding and acceptance of ideas drawn from psychoanalytic theory have caused some far-reaching changes in American attitudes toward the rearing and instruction of children. Recent changes in American education have grown, at least in part, out of an altered conception of what a child is, of how children should be expected to develop, and of how childhood is to be viewed by adults.

Psychoanalytic Images of the Child

From the seventeenth century down into the mid-1800's, Americans appear to have regarded children as miniature adults, incompetent and refractory, who needed to have good manners and useful information beaten into them and sinfulness beaten out. "Spare the rod and spoil the child," was a rule all but universally accepted.[1]

Gradually, men's minds changed; the child came to be thought of as a kind of exile from Heaven "trailing clouds of glory" which the experience of growing up darkened and then extinguished. Freud's exploration of the human psyche revealed an image of the child very different from either of these views. To cite Ernest Jones:

The images of the innocent babe or unfolding plant have been replaced by more sympathetic and living ones of creatures pathetically struggling "with no language but a cry" to achieve the self-control and inner security that civilized man has so far attempted in vain to attain. And the infant is urged to accomplish in five years of life what civilized adults have only imperfectly accomplished in a period ten thousand times as long.[2]

Jones implies that adults ask too much of the child. Freud goes further, declaring that the way in which children are trained depletes their minds. "Think of the distressing contrast between the radiant intelligence of a healthy child and the feeble mentality of the average adult."[3] Freud attributes this contrast, and the degeneration it suggests, to the early inculcation of religious doctrine and to the deliberate retardation of sexual development. Like women, Freud said, children, labored under the "harshness of the early prohibition which prevented them from applying their minds to what would have interested them most, that is to say, to the problems of sexual life."

Before turning to the impact of Freudian theory upon

[1] Margaret Mead and Martha Wolfenstein, eds., *Childhood in Contemporary Cultures* (Chicago: University of Chicago Press, 1955), p. 160.
[2] Ernest Jones, *Sigmund Freud: Four Centenary Addresses* (New York: Basic Books, Inc., 1956), p. 145.
[3] Sigmund Freud, *Future of an Illusion* (New York: Doubleday Anchor, 1957), p. 84.

formal instruction or upon child-rearing practices in the United States, let us look at some of the things analysts like Anna Freud and Melanie Klein have discovered about the patterns of children's psychological growth, and what implications their discoveries and concepts have for child rearing. Freud himself had observed and written about certain neurotic problems in children, but he did not work intensively with very young patients. It was Anna Freud, Melanie Klein, and their fellow workers who began the formal practice of child analysis in the 1920's, and it was then that techniques began to be developed for dealing with the very young child who showed indications of serious emotional disturbance.

Anna Freud used material drawn from her clinical experience with children as a basis for theories on the development of the ego, but we are not concerned with that aspect of her work here. During the late twenties and early thirties, Vienna had established a group of educational centers for neglected children and for the children of working mothers. In 1935, Anna Freud lectured to teachers at these special schools, outlining the psychoanalytic view of the course of child development and suggesting some application of those ideas to education. For, she said, psychoanalysis had made people aware that education "begins with [the] first day of life." Too often, parents secured obedience by threatening their children with punishment in terms that, to the child, implied bodily damage. Less brutal but as harmful in the long run was the parents' threat to withdraw their love. These techniques might help the parent change the "crying, troublesome and dirty infant" into the "well-behaved schoolchild" but often they secured the change at the price of "quenching the child's shrewdness and originality." It was necessary, she urged, to strike a balance, to allow the child gratification and to impose restrictions, each "in due proportion."

American parents who heard about the new theories of child development often lost sight of that due proportion, as we shall see, and in that loss may well lie one root of the identity problem which is so important a factor in the clini-

cal picture so many contemporary patients present in psychotherapy.

From her work with disturbed children, Anna Freud concluded that methods of teaching should be adapted to the
child's level of emotional growth as well as to his intellectual
capacity, that teachers should use analytic insights to improve
their understanding of themselves as well as of their pupils,
and that teachers should be particularly alert to signs that
a child needed psychotherapeutic help. It was especially necessary to ease children's fears so that they could be free to
work and to learn. And it was equally important for teachers
to understand their own unconscious conflicts so that they
would not victimize their pupils.[4]

Melanie Klein has made a noteworthy contribution to analytic technique, although she differs from the classicists on
points of theory; *play therapy*—the use of toys, water, pots
and pans, and the like, and the observation of the child employ-
ing them—is particularly associated with her name. Unlike
Anna Freud, Klein believed that it was possible to use true
analytic procedure rather than more specifically educational
methods in dealing with child patients. In her opinion, moreover, the child was not only a sexual being, but an exceedingly
anxious one, suffering from guilt roused by sadistic responses
to "the primal scene," to the birth of siblings, and to the
neuroses of his parents.

Thus, according to Klein, childhood was neither "pure"
nor "happy." The child was roused to guilt by fear of its own
pregenital impulses, particularly its desire to rend and destroy,
and by the demands of the parent whom it experienced as
stern and punitive. The child's hostilities, its fears and anxieties,
Klein contends, make it difficult to rear and equally difficult
to teach. For example, a child may think of learning as a means
of discovering what it is not supposed to know. Such discovery
is bound to rouse fear of punishment in the child; it is afraid
to learn and comes to feel that in stupidity lies safety. By

[4] Anna Freud, *Psychoanalysis for Teachers and Parents* (Boston:
Beacon, 1960), pp. 39, 77, 105, 106–14.

relieving the child's anxiety, psychoanalytic treatment may lessen the severity of the superego the child develops in response to its fear and guilt and so liberate him to become a more social being, pleasanter to live with at home, and easier to educate at school. Further, by recognizing and treating psychotic traits and character disorders while the child is young, psychoanalysis can prevent the warping of its growth. As Klein put it:

> If every child who shows disturbances that are at all severe were to be analysed in good time, a great number of those people who later end up in prisons or lunatic asylums, or who go completely to pieces, would be saved from such a fate and be able to develop a normal life. If Child Analysis can accomplish a work of this kind—and there are many indications that it can—it would be the means not only of helping the individual but of doing incalculable service to society as a whole.[5]

It is still true, decades after those words were written, that too little is being done in the United States to detect and to treat neurotic disturbances in young children. A number of people, however, have become convinced that children can suffer from neurosis, that they will not necessarily "grow out of" the disorder, and that the neurosis can be treated. At least the first steps have been made. Whether those steps will develop into a thoroughgoing program of preventive medicine in mental health is, like so many other issues raised by the diffusion of psychoanalytic ideas in education, a query only the future can answer.

In considering the effect of psychoanalysis on education in America, one must mention, at least in passing, Erik Erikson's important study of the relationship between the process of psychological maturation and the character of the society in which a child lives. Erikson's orientation is less clinical and more broadly cultural than either Anna Freud's or Klein's. Erikson takes a good deal of analytic theory as "given" and

[5] Melanie Klein, *Psychoanalysis of Children* (New York: Grove Press, 1960), pp. 36, 149, 374.

goes on to describe how a child learns to know and adapt to the demands of the particular cultural world into which he has been born. From his background in anthropology, Erikson drew the varied material he uses to give us a keener appreciation of the variety of cultural worlds and of the way in which each operates to shape the patterns of emotional response which the children born into it will show. Although *Childhood and Society* is no handbook of instruction for parents, it offers its readers useful insights into the changing needs of a growing child.

Education and Acculturation in America

Turning now to the more general question of the impact of psychoanalysis upon education in the United States, Americans, as we have noted, have long been concerned with education in a way that did not affect Europeans until quite recently. In Europe, any high level of formal education long remained a privilege of the prosperous. In England, and as late as the 1840's and 1850's, even the ability to read and write was regarded as an unsuitable accomplishment for the poor. A little learning was regarded as dangerous for the lower classes; the man who could read might demand higher wages and more leisure. In the United States, on the other hand, since the seventeenth century some measure of formal education has been regarded as necessary for all children; tax-supported, nonsectarian free schools have been the rule in the North and West since the late 1830's.

Further, when one recalls the millions of immigrants from different cultures who came to America between 1885 and 1920, one can see why the American approach to education should be so different from that common in the less fluid society of Europe: there is a huge distance between accepting a tradition and trying to develop one, between educating children to fit into a relatively stable society, and educating children to accept social mobility as their expected way of life. All education is acculturation; in every human society, the developing human infant must be "housebroken" to the culture. He must learn to satisfy his instinctual needs in ways that his culture will at least tolerate; he must learn to direct his basic drives into the channels his culture provides. In the United States, and particularly during the years between 1885 and 1925, the "housebreaking" process was the task of the school to a greater degree than was generally true in Europe. Indeed, the American public school became the accepted social instrument for transforming the immigrant child into an American. During his brief schooling (compulsory attendance at school until the age of fourteen or sixteen years did not become the rule in most states until late in the 1920's) the immigrant child had to acquire a new set of social imperatives. Moreover, it was taken for granted during these decades that this new culture was one which the child should wholeheartedly accept because the values to which he was being introduced were "higher" than those his parents had brought with them. He was encouraged to repudiate his past; customary patterns of authority were disrupted; established methods of achieving a sense of identity were depleted. Children were required to choose between worlds, as it were, and the divorce between parent and child which resulted has had important consequences for contemporary American society.

American educators, charged as they were with a task that went far beyond mere instruction in academic subjects and skills, were ready to seek help from any source. Although mental testing was in fact a European invention, the example of the Binet-Simon tests, first devised in the years 1905–1911, was followed with particular intensity in the United States, where the I.Q. became something of an educational fetish during the 1920's and afterward. (What had first been devised as a means of easing pressure on the dull child now became an instrument which tended to increase pressure on all children.) Educational psychology became an accepted part of the formal curriculum in teachers' education and—however diluted a discipline it may have been—such acceptance showed that the professional educators who hold so influential a position in

American school systems were ready to recognize and employ new tools.

Freud's influence in American education is often associated with that of John Dewey. One should recall, however, that the first experience in the kind of education Dewey favored occurred in the 1890's and early 1900's; they antedate the period of Freud's influence on even the most alert American educators. Still, Dewey's educational emphasis, shifting attention as it did from the classroom subject to the child, from school as preparation to school as a satisfying present experience, did much to open the way for Freudian thinking to affect the ideas of a number of American educators. Dewey's principal concern—to make formal education a more effective preparation for living by giving it meaning within the context of the child's own life—was not derived from Freudian theories about human development, but it was not opposed to those theories. Thus, a child-centered teacher who accepted Dewey's educational philosophy might well find common ground with educators who accepted the Freudian picture of the child's drives and patterns of growth.

Freudian Influence on Child Rearing

After the First World War, progressive methods in education became more acceptable to school administrators; but it was child rearing rather than school instruction that first responded to Freudian influence. In the twenties, particularly, superficial acquaintance with Freud's early work reinforced the notion that "self-expression" should be a goal of child training. Some of the ways in which a number of literary men accepted—and distorted—Freud's ideas have already been noted. A similar distortion contributed to the growth of a new attitude toward child rearing. Children have long held a peculiarly central place in American family life. Long before Freud's theories were popularized the American child was described as over-indulged, disrespectful of his elders and their authority, socially precocious, and intellectually undisciplined. During the 1920's, it was the most sophisticated parents, the people most rebellious against their own society and most receptive to new ideas—or most susceptible to new fads and most easily impressed by novel vocabularies—who acquired at least a smattering of psychoanalytic concepts and who applied that smattering to their children. These parents were inclined to harken when told that children's development could be stunted by rigorous discipline and that permissiveness, on the other hand, would foster a child's growth.

In the schools, too, it was the most sophisticated group that responded to Freudian theory. Disciples and exaggerators of Dewey's ideas urged that children be allowed to learn only what they wished to learn and at their own pace. It was assumed that children thus schooled would become aware of the gaps in their knowledge and would be eager to study and fill them when they saw the need. Popularizers of Freud reinforced this trend; they counseled parents and educators to avoid rigid discipline, judgmental attitudes, inflexible demands for accomplishment. During the decades before the First World War, both educators and parents had tended to make unreasonable demands on the young people in their care. Now, many shifted; instead of asking too much, they asked too little; especially on the intellectual level. The consequences of the change were not fully felt for more than a decade after the Great Depression of the early 1930's. Nor can these consequences be attributed only to the altered emphasis in education. More children were attending school; the new group of pupils had different purposes than had been common before the First World War, when fewer than half the secondary-school age group went to high school. Moreover, teaching these young people presented new problems, some of which might have been solved by a discriminating application of Freudian thinking. Unfortunately, however, the application has—then and now—but rarely been discriminating. Many school authorities have, in effect, given up the effort really to educate young people who were not preparing for college.

Instead, a number of them have employed certain Freudian concepts to bolster the development of a "life-adjustment" curriculum which substituted watered-down versions of English and social studies for substantial training either in vocational skills or in basic literacy.[6]

It is interesting to note that, during the 1920's, Freudian theory had a serious rival as a psychological fad in education in the stimulus-response behaviorism which John Watson adapted from Pavlov. Behaviorist studies in animal behavior and in learning theory were rather more common than experimental work with psychoanalytical concepts.[7] The behaviorists sometimes attacked psychoanalysis as thoroughly unscientific (a charge which other experimental psychologists supported), as merely another outmoded exercise in obsolete conceptions like "consciousness."

Goodwin Watson, the social psychologist, argues that however psychoanalysis may have influenced certain parents, it had little actual effect on primary and secondary schools during the 1920's. As evidence, he notes that among texts in educational psychology published during that decade, few spent more than four pages on describing unconscious factors in motivation. Prospective teachers using these could scarcely bring Freudian thought into the classroom. Not until the 1950's did the authors of educational psychology textbooks begin to devote as many as forty-six pages, on the average, to unconscious factors and their impact on learning. Similarly, textbooks of a generation ago gave mental hygiene only about

[6] Indeed, it might be argued that many contemporary young people are in secondary school for no purpose of their own; they are there because the law requires attendance. Edgar Z. Friedenberg in *Coming of Age in America* (New York: Random House, 1965, p. 42), makes the point that although the adolescent is obliged to attend school the community recognizes no correlative obligation that the school make any return; he is, in effect, committed (as a convict to jail or an emotionally disturbed person to a mental hospital).

[7] Shakow and Rapoport, "The Influence of Freud on American Psychology," *Psychological Issues*, Monograph 13, 1964, pp. 167–70, point out that formally designed experiments to test Freudian concepts were not undertaken on any considerable scale until the 1930's.

seven pages; now they devote more than fifty pages to the topic. And even those current texts which do not cite Freud sprinkle their paragraphs with terms like "rationalization," "displaced hostility," "self-punishment," "repression," "fantasy," and "compulsiveness."

The upsurge of interest in Freud among educators may be attributed to a return of the focus of attention to the individual and his problems after the Depression decade of the thirties and the war years, when economic and social issues and then national survival seemed of primary importance. The strain of war and postwar readjustment intensified awareness of emotional problems. Perhaps desire to escape from effort to deal with what seemed insoluble social issues also influenced the resurgence of interest in psychoanalysis so evident in the late forties and the fifties. In the field of education as elsewhere, the more familiar Freudian theory became, the more it seemed to be diluted. It is interesting to compare the view of the child as described in United States Children's Bureau Publications in 1914 and the view in publications on the same topic in the late forties. The child in 1914, before Freud had made much impression, was described as a creature of great energy whose impulses were in need of forcible restraint: thumbsucking was to be discouraged by methods of torture—for instance, actually tying the child's arm in such a way that he could not put his thumb into his mouth. In 1945, after psychoanalysis had become familiar to many educated people, the child's impulses were described as far less urgent; he was a distractible creature who could be diverted from masturbating, say, by an abundance of toys; and he need not be restrained from sucking his thumb at all.[8]

To distortions of the latter kind, watering down the stern realism with which Freud looked at the human personality, we may attribute some of the failures of contemporary education. So far as attitudes toward child training are concerned, the child has been more encouraged to express himself than helped

[8] Mead and Wolfenstein, *op. cit.*, pp. 170–77; 444.

to develop an identity, a self he can express. A garbled version
of Freud's early work was taken to justify extreme permissiveness. It is rather easy to interpret the trend toward indulgence
in terms of reaction from Victorian restraints. Whereas parents
of earlier generations had been regarded as virtuous because,
and insofar as, they forbade their children any pleasure that had
not been "earned" by obedience and hard work, now parents
were good when they provided continuous gratification for the
child. Ironically, American parents and teachers discovered
the id just as Freud's own interests were shifting to other areas
of the psyche.[9] Popularizers and interpreters ignored or mini-
mized his later work which emphasizes the organizing and integrating functions of the ego. However, as Freud pointed out,
the ego does not develop automatically; it matures in response
to the boundaries which parental discipline lays down for the
child and which serve to help him develop an awareness and
acceptance of the reality which is constituted by other people
and by the social world as a whole. The most useful reaction
against the crippling restrictiveness of Victorian methods of
child rearing is not unqualified license (a permissiveness which
sometimes seems to resemble refusal to accept the parental
role). Rather, rigid restrictiveness needs to be replaced by
flexible and well informed discipline which establishes suitable
restraints and gradually modifies these until young people can
be genuinely independent. However, as therapists like Harry
F. Tashman have remarked, many parents use their children as
vehicles through which they can compensate for their own
childhood's unappeased hungers. When such parents lavish
toys and toy-surrogates like cars upon their children, they
give to themselves; and at times, sincerely believing that they
give with love, these parents actually give in jealousy, resent-
ing what they do for their children because it was not done
for them.[10]

[9] Charles Rolo, ed., *Psychiatry in American Life* (Boston: Little,
Brown, 1963), p. 135.
[10] Harry F. Tashman, *Today's Neurotic Family* (New York: University Publishers, Inc., 1960), p. 179.

As a result of the percolation of Freudian ideas throughout American society, parents and even children have acquired a degree of psychological sophistication. Adolescents are familiar with psychological jargon. More important, they seem to be far more sensitive to changes in adult attitudes toward them than were young people in earlier generations; perhaps, since adult attitudes seem to change more rapidly, such sensitivity is necessary for survival.

Contemporary American children are probably the first children in the history of the world who must, on a very nearly conscious level, relate to their mothers and fathers not only as parents but also as peers, sometimes even as competitors: the mother appears as competing with her daughter for the father's love; the father as son's rival for the mother's attention. Parents, in their turn, are aware of a changing relation to their children. Often they feel suspended between the inner-directed character structure, which they still retain in some measure, and the other-directed character type, which they have encouraged their children to develop. American life has for a long time chipped away at the unquestioned authority of the parent as parent; and fathers and mothers today are not generally willing to stand or struggle against a change that they largely accept, emotionally, even as it makes them uncomfortable. Parents who are thus uncertain can scarcely serve as useful guides for their children.

In many middle-class homes, emotional relationships have been made a conscious center of family life, just as they have been brought into the classrooms of many of our better schools. (The slum school and the lower-class family have changed, too, perhaps, but adequate studies of these segments of society are not available in sufficient number to permit useful generalization.[11]) The child's emotional life has been made

[11] It might be argued that the children of the poor, who comprise an increasing proportion of the population of our central cities, need to be initiated into the majority culture, and that the teacher who emphasizes her role of parent-surrogate may be best able to help in the task of acculturation. The social distance between the middle-class young woman and her lower-class pupils is often too great to allow her

increasingly self-conscious; indeed many prosperous parents seem to agree with Melanie Klein and to consider neurosis as part of the psychological makeup of their children. This trend has provoked Rollo May to write that "psychoanalysis and psychotherapy [may well become] part of the neurosis of our day rather than part of the cure."[12]

Psychoanalysis and the Educational Revolution

The increased interest in psychology and psychoanalysis (occurring as it did at about the very time that the educational system was being expected to prepare an increasing number of students for life in an increasingly difficult world) has operated to produce a revolution in American education. To cite John Seeley again, this revolution is both external and internal, affecting both methods of teaching and, as has been shown, the most private aspects of a child's orientation in life.[13]

Insights derived from psychoanalysis can and sometimes have been used to free children of anxiety—so that they do not, for example, think of learning as a threatening activity. But misapprehension of psychoanalytic concepts has caused serious damage to formal education in America. Both Dewey's emphasis on the child as the proper center of the school and Freud's dynamic theory of the child as father of the (too often neurotic) man have been used to thin the content of instruction and to slow its pace. The child, it is argued, should not be required to do anything difficult, he should always succeed at

---

to take on the role very effectively even if she should have reasonably adequate training in the psychology of child development. The classroom that most needs an atmosphere of warmth and acceptance as a precondition for formal learning is least likely to get it—unless increased awareness of the need can somehow inspire a willingness to fill it. The need is becoming more and more generally recognized, however, and that recognition in itself bears witness to the penetration of psychoanalytic concepts into the thinking of some professional educators.

[12] Charles Rolo, ed., *op. cit.*, p. 37.

[13] John R. Seeley, "The Americanization of the Unconscious," in Hendrik M. Ruitenbeek, ed., *Psychoanalysis and Social Science* (New York: Dutton, 1962), pp. 186–87.

what he attempts; he should not be pushed to stretch his mind. He should not, for instance, be expected to read any but condensed and simplified versions of literary classics because he should not be exposed to educational material outside the limited range of experience which can be meaningful to him. Such deliberate narrowing of exposure (a narrowing said to be fostered by certain techniques in the teaching of reading), coupled with renewed emphasis on grades in many schools, tends to make students dependent on abridgements, digests, and handbooks and encourages them to avoid contact with the primary text.

Exaggeration of valid observations—for example, that children study more willingly and more effectively if they are confronted with standards adapted to their own capacities and if they have reasonably frequent experience of success—helps account for what might be called a general retardation. Teachers at every level of instruction report that they must deal with topics they might reasonably expect pupils to have mastered earlier.

Ironically, although the individual child is said to be the object of attention and although his individual development is the stated center of educational concern, he is continuously being tested, graded, ranged along statistical frequency curves, and so assigned a place in respect to others rather than in respect to a more impersonal criterion. Where he stands often seems more important than what level of mastery that standing represents. The content of instruction is being depleted (except perhaps in the mathematics and physical science taught the exceptionally able youngster), a trend particularly evident in urban public schools. Yet, at the same time, we hear demands that the school and the teacher take on a responsibility which no school should be expected to assume. The educational system is being asked to supply the child with the understanding, the "therapeutic environment" which neither parents nor the rest of society seem prepared to provide.

In many schools, and especially, perhaps, in those better schools in prosperous areas, the faculty appears to behave as if its chief function were to understand children rather than to help them acquire information and learn how to think realistically. The teacher may be more efficient when such understanding is part of his equipment; it is useful for him to interpret a child's behavior in terms of what that child is revealing about himself rather than in terms of moral absolutes which justify punishment for inattentiveness, unruliness, or failure to learn. And teachers who must impart facts—and who hope to impart some love of learning to their pupils—may profit from the fresh ideas which have been developed from the work of analysts like Hartmann and Federn. But all this is, in large part, instrumental. If education does not seek to expand and develop the intellect, if it has nothing but so-called life adjustment as a goal, and if that life adjustment is defined as acceptance of the imperative "Be a good consumer" in something taken to be the best of all possible worlds, then the role of psychoanalysis in education must be regarded with some misgiving.

Too many teachers are uncritical in accepting the role of parent-surrogate. Of course, it is helpful for the teacher to know that the child may see her as a mother (or even a father) figure and react to her accordingly. It is useful for her to be aware of how such a reaction can interfere with formal learning. It even may be helpful for teachers to observe and understand the behavior of children in the classroom in terms of what John Seeley calls the "depth drama" underlying every act. But the teacher should not become so involved in watching this drama and studying relationships between the children she is teaching that she neglects the classroom's other reason for existence; namely, helping children learn to handle the intellectual tools which give them command of important aspects of their culture.

Psychoanalysis and the Higher Learning

In colleges and universities, psychology and psychoanalysis play an ambiguous role. The psychological counselor is a familiar figure at many schools. Teacher training, which European educational systems generally relegate to lower levels than the university, receives considerable attention in American institutions of higher learning (a large number of doctorates, for example, are granted in the field of education). In the curriculum for training teachers, much attention is devoted to educational methods and to educational psychology. A portion of this instruction is in learning theory and techniques for conveying information and persuading children to accept it, but increasingly, teacher training is giving attention to processes of psychological development and to personality mechanisms which may hinder the teacher in her understanding of those processes. Sometimes, the boundaries between treatment and instruction become blurred. The same department will offer instruction in group dynamics and sessions in group therapy.[14] The consequent failure of students to distinguish between the two tends to build resistance to therapy without a corresponding increase of intellectual understanding.

Increased psychological sophistication has additional perils at the college level. Students often feel quite prepared to "analyze" each other. Although damage is possible, it is doubtful if any but the very disturbed young person could be seriously injured by such amateur "head-shrinking." More troublesome, from a clinical viewpoint, is the student who comes into therapy with a tongue made glib from attending a few psychology courses or reading a few books by Erich Fromm or even by Freud himself. Such patients may intellectualize their problems to a degree that hampers progress in treatment. Yet the contemporary analyst, recalling the prevalence of hysteria in the nineteenth century, may acquire from his experience with such students greater understanding of how each period brings its own socially generated distractions and distortions to the therapeutic encounter.

The college student who has embraced sexual promiscuity as a way of life—and discusses that embrace in psychological

[14] Practice at The College of the City of New York is a case in point.

jargon—may be far less free than his talk or his conduct would indicate. "Promoting maturity" is often the stated objective of educators and educational administrators; yet a look at the regulations of most colleges makes one wonder if those who proclaim that objective have any idea what it means. The high school student, who usually lives at home, is often allowed much liberty. If he has a part-time job, his parents generally allow him to spend his earnings as he chooses; they do not usually keep close watch over his comings and goings. But when the same young person goes away to college, he finds himself governed by a restraining parent-substitute. At a time when he should be encouraged to experiment, to make his own decisions, and to accept responsibility for their outcome, the student is put into a straitjacket of regulations. Newspapers still make headlines of purported sexual misbehavior among college students. And if those students are girls, the headlines are the more sensational and titillating to readers who have not been to college and envy those who have.

Young people moving from high school into college often move from liberty to restriction and from a low level of academic expectation to one that is bewilderingly higher. In high school the young person is free to do as he chooses socially, and classroom requirements are equally undemanding. For despite the post-Sputnik clamor and the very real competition and tension generated by effort to get into "prestige" colleges, many American high schools still ask their students to learn very little. State law compels many state universities to admit any local high school graduate who applies. Even colleges with more selective admission policies accept students whose academic records are less than distinguished. We are even beginning to hear protest against a "new snobbery" not of the purse but of the intellect. Still and all, most colleges demand that the students they do admit perform at college level, and the abrupt change in expectation often has a traumatic effect, even on intellectually able people.

Here, for all the abundance of psychological counseling, we see that traditional educational practice has not been as deeply affected by psychoanalysis as might be hoped. Some educators continue to resist Freudian insights. Others merely ignore what application of those insights could do for their students. Unfortunately, the American young person does not necessarily flourish psychologically on the material achievements of his society alone, notable as those have been. According to the dean of an important American woman's college—and the women's colleges are often more selective and demanding than men's schools of equivalent standing—insecure and materialistic parents cannot give their children workable standards of sexual behavior or even proper health habits, let alone useful educational goals.[15] The same dynamism that contributes so much to American economic achievement also contributes to the instability, social and individual, which has so greatly intensified students' emotional problems. These problems are evident in the attitudes of students toward the marriages they enter so readily and as readily dissolve. They are evident, too, in the attitudes of students toward their work. Some become excessively competitive and anxious. Others drop out, yet continue to live near the schools they have left, refusing either to prepare for the practical life of the adult world or to enter it on an appropriate level, thus repudiating its standards and demands.

The prevalence and gravity of situations of this kind make it urgent that the academic community as a whole rethink its attitude toward the psychological condition of its student members. This portion of society is, ironically, all but saturated with the jargon of psychoanalysis. Colleges and universities express concern about students' psychological well-being; they sometimes provide personnel and programs intended to help individual students; yet they direct little attention to the general problem. Perhaps it is unrealistic to expect that they do so, since the general problem of the student's attitude toward himself and his work is so intricately intertwined with the

[15] The Dean of Barnard implied that an appreciable number of contemporary students have been reared by such parents. (*A History of Barnard College* [New York: The College, 1964], p. 110.)

situation of society as a whole. Nevertheless, it seems that universities (and school systems as a whole) might devote more careful thought to their programs of psychological counseling. They might then apply psychoanalytic insights more effectively and so make their programs more useful in furthering the larger purpose of helping students become more independent persons with more secure identities while they are acquiring their formal general education.

6 · Freud and Religion

6 · Freud and Religion

ON May 6, 1956, the hundredth anniversary of Freud's birth, psychoanalysts, psychologists, and clergymen gathered at the cathedral of St. John the Divine in New York to honor the founder of psychoanalysis. The author of *Wit and the Unconscious* would have enjoyed the irony of the occasion. For Freud considered religion to be an expression of man's irrational drives, a kind of obsessional neurosis descending by social example through the generations, and he used what is currently labeled the *Judaeo-Christian tradition* as his paradigm of religion.

Freud's Theory of Religion

Freud's ideas on religion are to be found in *Totem and Taboo* (1913), in *The Future of an Illusion* (1927), and in *Moses and Monotheism* (1939). The first, using anthropological authorities like Robertson Smith, who were even then considered somewhat out of date, traced human culture to "man's first disobedience and the Fall." That is, Freud told how the sons had banded together against authority; how they had killed the father—the Old Man of the horde—and gained access to the women he had kept for himself. By eating what they had killed, the sons took the Old Man's power into themselves. Then, repenting the crime, to ease the pain of guilt and anxiety and to prevent the crime's repetition, they created human culture: they would not kill and they would not seek women, at least within the clan or tribe; they would control aggression and avoid incest. And, at stated intervals, solemnly, they would gather to eat the surrogate of the murdered father's body, the sacred animal, the totem, which otherwise was a forbidden meat. *Totem and Taboo* had been concerned with primitives and had created what might be called a "social myth" in the style of the "social contract"; in the *Future of an Illusion* and *Moses and Monotheism* Freud dealt with more modern aspects of religion. Modern religion had its roots in the helplessness of man before nature, in the demands of the culture, and in the carrying into adult life of the child's experience and his attitudes toward that experience. The child sees the father as powerful, threatening, but inscrutable and, in undependable fashion, beneficent. The man has made his god in that image.

In *Moses and Monotheism* Freud addressed himself to the religion of his own tradition. Moses was an Egyptian, Freud declared, a leader slain by those he had led.[1] The descendants of those who had murdered him made Moses Prophet of the One God, the father whom he had figured and defined (perhaps as an adherent of the monotheistic, ethically oriented Aton cult which had been briefly triumphant and then suppressed in Egypt). The Hebrews had again taken up the faith of the man they murdered after a period in which they had abandoned that religion for one centering around a volcano-god, limited, vindictive, and primitive. The Pentateuch records the attempt to reconcile the two faiths and weave them into one; the joining appears in inconsistencies that make one aware of the dual presence.

By making Moses an Egyptian and the Hebrew faith an offshoot of that which the Egyptian king Ikhnaton had professed, Freud struck at the pride of the Jews; he threw into question the very source of their religion and of the peoples whose scriptures depended for authority on the inspiration of

[1] *Moses and Monotheism* (New York: Vintage, 1955), pp. 17, 57.

the Hebrew Bible, including Christians. The Jews glorified the father and praised him forever; they claimed the place of chosen children and denied that they had participated in the primal crime. The Christians admitted their guilt, but they worshipped the son—descendant of the rebellious leader of those first murderers who had driven the father from his place.[2] By virtue of his death, however, the Christian son not only became equal to the father but achieved equality in a way which allayed guilt. The peoples of Northern Europe, later converted to a monotheism they never wholeheartedly accepted, tended to project their dislike of that faith onto the Jews who adhered to monotheism in its most rigid form.[3]

Freud contended then that human culture had been developed at a high cost in guilt and anxiety. To maintain culture, men must continuously forego gratification: they must accept frustration of sexual desire and they must restrain aggressiveness. Moreover, material civilization can exist only if most men are compelled to endure deprivation; coercion alone can make them work and do without in order to accumulate the surpluses that allow other men to live with less labor and so to create law, art, and learning. For until very recently in the history of man, if wealth was to be produced and accumulated, the great body of humankind had to accept privation and hard labor.

Obviously, men do renounce instinctual gratification. Obviously, too, most men accept the need to work hard for a generally meager living although they see other men enjoying material goods without working. And most men do not require too much external compulsion to make them refrain from murder and incest. Are men then, as the Enlightenment contended, naturally good, ready to sacrifice themselves to the common welfare?

Freud acknowledges the sacrifice but argues that men make it only because they develop within themselves a defender of the culture, a guardian of property and the proprieties (it

[2] *Ibid.*, p. 111.
[3] *Ibid.*, p. 117.

would perhaps be more formal to call them the *mores*). This inner agent of enforcement he called the superego, and he described how the child achieves internalization of these commands of his culture, how he thus comes to accept the frustration and the privation which life in civilization exacts of him.

"For the individual as for mankind," Freud writes, "life is hard to endure."[4] Nature threatens; culture deprives; and men are more aware of threat and deprivation than of their converse, the nurturing potentialities of the world and of society. The world confronts men with barren soil, disease, the fury of storm, and the certainty of death. Against these evils, most men were helpless. But men could see these evils as the work of supernatural persons and that gave hope. For people can be obeyed; they can be bribed; they can be appeased.

Thus the gods came into being, in the image of the father. As nature is observed to operate impersonally, the gods concern themselves more with morality and less with celestial mechanics. They establish a moral order in the universe, a moral order, incidentally, which supports the requirements of the culture: that men accept instinctual frustration and material privation without becoming troublesomely rebellious. For existence of the moral order makes it possible to say that everything which occurs expresses the purpose of a superior being who, in ways we do not understand "orders everything for good, that is, to our advantage."[5]

Freud defines religion as ". . . certain dogmas, assertions about facts and conditions of external (or internal) reality, which tell one something that one has not oneself discovered and which claim that one should give them credence."[6] The dogmas are to be believed because they are ancient; they can be proved, and they ought not to be questioned, in any case. But, Freud remarks, antiquity of a belief testifies to the probable ignorance of the believer; the proofs of the Western

[4] *Future of an Illusion* (New York: 1957, Doubleday Anchor), p. 24.
[5] *Ibid.*, p. 29.
[6] *Ibid.*, p. 41.

religion are contained in a revelation which can be validated only from within itself, and refusal to allow examination of a claim is itself an admission of its weakness.

Yet the dogmas are believed (and will continue to be believed, perhaps). Belief rests not on the validity of arguments or real evidence advanced in its support but on the dogmas' fulfilling the "oldest, strongest and most insistent wishes of mankind." Ideas derived from the desire to have wishes gratified are illusions. Freud acknowledged that reason could not refute religous doctrines, but those doctrines could not be shown to give any information about external reality.[7] In defending religious dogma, people were ready to misrepresent their opponents and to deceive themselves. They called a man most truly religious when he was most stricken by conviction that before the majesty of the universe, he was as nothing. Such humility, in Freud's opinion, constituted an abjection unworthy of an adult. The man who accepted his impotence without the effective protest represented by effort to learn what reality was and how to deal with it was for Freud, indeed, *ir*religious, for such a man denied his bond to reality. (The word "religion," it will be remembered, comes from the Latin root meaning "to bind.")

Mankind as a whole, Freud maintained, has experienced something resembling the obsessional neurosis of childhood, which develops because the child (since he can deal with his impulses in no other way) represses forbidden instinctual impulses in order that he will not vent them in action. Men's religious behavior recalls this tendency of childhood; hence religion can be understood as "the universal obsessional neurosis of humanity."[8]

The heart of Freud's argument is that truth is the understanding of external reality (including man's mental life) and that science is the only road to truth.[9] By implication, truth in the long run is more rewarding than any psychological

[7] *Ibid.*, pp. 54, 55.
[8] *Ibid.*, p. 78.
[9] *Ibid.*, p. 102.

comfort to be had from a view of the universe that does not correspond to reality.

The Churches and Psychoanalysis: Rejection

Freud expected that psychoanalysis would be repugnant to believers. They could scarcely welcome any line of thought which defined religion as a kind of collective neurosis and treated religionists' convictions about the power of their deity and the truth of their doctrines as a psychotherapist might treat a neurotic obsession in an individual patient.[10]

Moreover, in the United States, Freud's views on infantile sexuality were especially offensive. Most Protestants had given up the early Puritan emphasis on infant depravity and replaced it with more or less refined versions of the sentimental cult of the child. To assert the existence of sexuality in little children, who by definition were pure, was peculiarly objectionable to clergymen in a culture deeply committed to the belief that sex was dirty. The notion of sex as a filthy distraction diverting men's attention from the pursuit of money is one aspect of what is called puritanism. This attitude was common among American Catholics, too, for the Roman Church in the United States has, on the whole, been dominated by its Irish members, who are deeply imbued with the puritan *mores* of their traditional enemy. Prudery and intense concern with keeping one's neighbors moral are common among Christian denominations in the United States, and psychoanalysis is no friend of prudery.

In the 1920's, particularly, when American social standards were changing so rapidly, clerical opposition to psychoanalysis concentrated on its presumed encouragement of sexual "looseness." When men asked for help in dealing with their sexual problems, the churches had little to offer beyond Paul's "It is better to marry than burn." Since the 1920's, many

[10] *Moses and Monotheism*, p. 68.

Protestant sects have taken a somewhat more permissive position, but others continue bound to a narrow understanding of an old sex morality. Roman Catholicism, too, has maintained a generally rigid outlook. In Europe, so far as male behavior is concerned, Catholicism has usually been fairly permissive in respect to sex; in the United States, the Church is often indistinguishable from the most puritanical of Protestant groups. Both sects tend to be concerned with effort to keep the public mind pure of contamination by improper books, magazines, and motion pictures. Both often lack genuine understanding of people's sexual problems; they denigrate sexuality and define morality as the abstention from sexual activity outside the bonds of marriage.

In the 1920's, the evangelical sects denounced Freud along with Darwin. The age was wicked; the intellectuals who accepted the theory of evolution and the principles of psychoanalysis bore witness to the prevalence of corruption. Catholic opinion may have been as hostile to intellectual innovation but it expressed its hostility less noisily. It was Protestant groups that took legal action against Darwinism in Tennessee and the several other states that forbade the public high schools to teach the theory of evolution. They attacked Darwinism rather than psychoanalysis partly because it contradicted Scripture forthrightly, but also partly because psychology was not taught in the secondary schools; and hence opposition to Freudian thought could not readily take the form of hostile legal action.

During the 1930's, the churches' antagonism to psychoanalysis tended to flag as the Depression turned the attention of all America to economic problems: neurosis and the suffering it entailed seemed insignificant in comparison to the pain of going hungry.

The Second World War and the decade which followed brought analysis to a new position in American life, and that new position engendered a new and perhaps more serious form of opposition to Freudian thought. As custodians of the society's spiritual values, clergymen began to express their concern with the impact of Freud's ideas on such religious concepts as guilt, sin, and responsibility, the nature of conscience and the function of introspection. Freud maintained that childhood experience was determinative of adult attitudes, determinative in ways not available to consciousness. As Gregory Zilboorg—repeating Freud in other language—pointed out in 1939, the discovery of the role of the unconscious threatened men's narcissism, their attachment to, and overvaluation of, themselves.[11] The demonstration of the large part that unconscious mechanisms play in creating and maintaining religious faith seemed to taint the very source of belief. Specifically, if people's conduct was guided by their emotions, if even the attempt to control emotion was an emotional phenomenon, and if emotions were determined by unconscious factors, how could any man be held responsible for his thoughts and his acts?

The analyst sought to free patients of bondage to a punitive superego; the clergyman was committed in greater or less degree to encouraging his parishioners to accept the rectitude of their superego's commands. For, to the clergyman, the voice of conscience was the voice of God, not the internalized commands of parents and of society as that was reflected by parental order, and it was man's duty to heed and obey that voice. The analyst sought to free men from the pain of irrational guilt: a man's wicked thoughts did no one any harm. A child's feeling guilty because he did not know how to handle instinctual impulses—which he must indeed learn not to express in action—could poison all a man's life. But many clergymen accepted as truth some version of the doctrine that men, by their nature, were guilty of offending God: a man's wicked thoughts showed that he was capable of acting wickedly; a child's instinctual impulses gave further evidence that human nature was weak and that man was born prepared for corruption. God had provided a means by which men could atone for their offenses against God, but only by being aware of

[11] Gregory Zilboorg, *Psychoanalysis and Religion* (New York: Farrar, Straus and Cudahy, 1962).

their guilt and by being made anxious about it could they be impelled to seek and find the redemption which He had made possible.

Confronted with Freudian theory, spokesmen for religion could assume one of two postures: they could denounce psychoanalysis or they could seek to assimilate it. Repudiation was the initial response, and this continued to prevail, with greater or less intensity, into the 1940's, more perhaps among the Catholic clergy than the Protestant. Spokesmen for Judaism appear to have been less troubled by psychoanalysis. Some of them may have regarded *Moses and Monotheism* as a manifestation of disloyalty to the group, but they do not seem to have felt their belief discredited by it or their religious faith attacked. Orthodox Judaism is concerned with practicing its tradition, not with defending its originality or even its divine inspiration. Reform Judaism is concerned with present ethics rather than with the authenticity of historical claims. Thus neither of the main currents in American Judaism was especially concerned with combating psychoanalysis because neither felt especially threatened by Freud's attitude toward religion or by analytic therapy's focus on relieving irrational guilt.

This attitude was not shared by Catholic opinion. To cite one instance, the then Monsignor Sheen—in his very popular *Peace of Soul* (1949)—attacked psychoanalysis. Analytic treatment, he argued, was calculated to lead patients to deny the existence of God and the necessity for ethical behavior.[12]

In the *Future of an Illusion*, Freud had indeed declared that it was dangerous to base morality upon religious sanctions. He thought that as scientific information was diffused, belief in God would inevitably lessen among the lower classes, who were essentially hostile to culture, i.e., to ethical behavior. If morality actually were merely obedience to commands of God, then a weakened belief in God would indeed undermine the foundations of morality; the dangerous classes would become

[12] See Alan Keenan, *Neurosis and Sacraments* (New York: Sheed and Ward, 1950).

more dangerous. But Freud had long insisted that morality had
a more solid basis; not "an external world order" but the
"inescapable exigencies of human co-habitation" required men
to deal justly with one another. If people hostile to culture
would not act according to a morality that was self-evidently
necessary, it was unlikely that their religious belief would
make them behave better.

The events of the thirties did nothing to strengthen Freud's
belief in man's capacity to recognize reality by behaving de-
cently toward one another. In *Moses and Monotheism*, he
wrote: "We find with astonishment that progress has concluded an alliance with barbarism." Soviet Russia had been a
discouraging example of the distortion of high purposes. Hence
it was "a real weight off the heart to find in the case of the
German people that retrogression into prehistoric barbarism
can come to pass independently of any progressive idea."

Whereas Monsignor Sheen denounced psychoanalysis as
godless and immoral in rather general terms, other Catholic
writers found it unacceptable because they considered its
psychological determinism to deny the freedom of man's will
or because they thought analytic treatment substituted the
couch for the confessional.

Hostility to analysis is not universal among American Catholics, of course. As the Catholic population has risen into the
middle class, it has been increasingly exposed both to higher
education, often in nondenominational schools, and to the pressures of middle-class life. What is acceptable to that class as
a whole cannot be entirely rejected by American Catholics,
who are as subject to the influence of other-direction as their
non-Catholic fellows. Curiously, although psychoanalysis has
less general currency among Europeans than among Americans, it seems to have aroused greater intellectual interest
among Continental Catholics than among their American co-
religionists.[13] Thomist scholars in France and Belgium (as well
as in Canada) are at work trying to make Freud palatable to

[13] Zilboorg, *Freud and Religion* (Westminster, Md.: Newman Press,
1962), p. 5.

the Church. The relative indifference of American Catholics to such efforts at intellectual reconciliation in the United States is another indication of the powerful impact of American culture on the Church. As American analysts are generally less interested in the theoretical aspects of psychoanalysis than their European colleagues, so American Catholic clergymen are probably less concerned with what might be termed pure theology and its relationship to modern psychology and philosophy than are their European counterparts.[14] In other words, the "national genius" (if one may use so old-fashioned a phrase) is not hospitable to work which contributes to the *theory* rather than to the *technique* of a discipline, whether that discipline be psychotherapy or theology.

Among Protestants as among Catholics, the initial response to psychoanalysis was hostile. Freudian theory was considered to undermine faith and to threaten morality. It tried to show that human behavior was the inevitable outcome of the conflict between the individual's instinctual drives and the way in which he had been made to deal with those drives. Such psychological determinism contradicted man's moral freedom. It appeared, at least, to make nonsense of any demand that men accept responsibility for what they might do. Psychoanalysis denied that sexuality was wicked; it did not agree that current standards of sexual morality were either immutable or right. Acceptance of Freud's ideas would give libertinism a scientific license. Freud traced both the concept of deity and the power of religious sanctions to the infant's overestimation of his parents. By reducing conscience from the voice of God to the promptings of a superego which was no more than the internalized voice of the parent, men would have no guide but would be turned loose into a moral jungle. Further, the examination of one's motives encouraged, indeed required, by psychoanalytic therapy could not but lead to an unhealthy preoccupation with self.

Later, in the 1950's, the grounds of attack on psychoanalysis

[14] Michael Novak, "American Catholicism and the Council," *Commentary*, 40 (August, 1965), pp. 50–58.

were shifted. Its threat to religious orthodoxy was emphasized less than its impact on behavior. Psychoanalysis declared that the recognition of reality was the prime duty of man. Part of the reality to be recognized was the instinctive aggressiveness of the human being. By explaining the origins of moral standards, psychoanalysis had undercut the authority of those standards. Men reared in a competitive society, which was part of the reality they had to recognize, and taught to accept self-assertion by psychoanalysis, would recognize no moral barriers against aggressive pursuit of selfish ends.

The Church and Psychoanalysis: Rapprochement

Nevertheless, after the initial burst of hostility (which had come especially from conservative evangelical groups) many Protestant clergymen adopted a second means of confronting Freudian thought, i.e., reconciliation through assimilation. We have seen earlier how Americans attenuated Freud's appraisal of reality. Men, in his view, stand alone in an unheeding universe; they must struggle against nature for bread and against those drives within the self which are forever childish, forever encumbered by the neuroses which are the all but inevitable consequence of the attempt to live within human culture. Against the power of the physical world and the weakness of human nature, men have only their reason, the "mind" which Freud respected but whose influence he certainly did not overestimate, whether within the individual or the group.

As American therapists diminished the starkness of that view or asserted that it was not a necessary part of psychoanalysis, religion and psychoanalysis moved toward their present, generally amicable relationship. Freud's studies in the origin and nature of religion were not pursued to any great extent. His attacks on faith and his faith in science seemed a bit out-of-date in a consensual society where it was increasingly bad form for anyone to call another's convictions into question. After 1945, analysis was becoming another middle-class activity, and since religion stood in high social esteem,[15] it was only to be expected that analysts would minimize Freud's definition of religion as a neurosis. Some among the orthodox denied that analysis was concerned with values at all; psychoanalysis was merely a form of treatment designed to relieve emotional suffering. Freud's ideas about the development and elimination of a neurosis were to be accepted; what he chose to believe or not to believe about the moral order of the universe had nothing to do with psychoanalysis. Other analysts wrestled with their souls in print: they could not accept conventional religion as true, in the scientific sense, yet they could not forego it either. Perhaps truth could be redefined. Still others preferred to redefine religion. These excluded from "religion" what might be considered neurotic and then pointed out that psychoanalysis, of course, supported this kind of religion as conducive to emotional health. A fourth group carried the war into the enemy camp: irreligion was a neurotic phenomenon.

The clergy could not find too much satisfaction in such a definition of religion as Erich Fromm's, for he described it as a common orientation and a common object of devotion. This definition might apply to any faith; it did not even

[15] Shifting attitudes toward religion among intellectuals are illustrated by the curricula of many nondenominational colleges: today they offer a major in religion; thirty years ago, students often had to turn to their university's divinity school for courses in the Bible or in church history. Kierkegaard's popularity is another case in point, as is the interest in neo-orthodox writers like Richard Niebuhr and Paul Tillich and the concern with theological problems as contrasted with the "social gospel" approach (the struggle for civil rights may make this less applicable to future decades than it was during the 1950's).

If we turn to the larger community, we see that in a state like Missouri, only the banker outranked the clergyman in public esteem; and among housewives and the lower-income groups, even the banker took second place. (Data from a survey made in 1953 by the Missouri Bar Association, which was trying to find out how the public rated lawyers as compared with bankers, business executives, and members of the other professions. The Association decided the legal profession needed to polish its image a bit. See tables in *A Manual of Practice for Lawyers* [Englewood Cliffs, N.J.: Prentice-Hall, Inc., 1964]).

recognize theism as essential, much less present a coherent view of the universe and man's place in it. The real issue was the relationship between psychoanalysis and a religious neo-orthodoxy which claimed the field for a specific version of Christianity, in no intolerant way, of course.

The brutal events of the thirties and the experience of the Second World War, followed as they were by the realization of the significance of atomic weapons, brought many people to a new belief in original sin. After the holocaust, it was harder than ever to believe in the perfectibility of man. With the erosion of European power in the world, many of those whose optimism actually rested on the evident triumph of Western civilization found it more difficult than ever to be-lieve that the whole Creation moved toward perfection except in some dimension out of time. If salvation through religious faith was problematical, man's capacity to save himself seemed no more plausible. For whatever else men could control, they could not, or so it was argued, govern their own destructive drives. They needed something outside themselves to make them behave and to give them a sense that their lives had meaning.

More and more people tried to find that meaning in the faith of the churches they joined. The churches for their part—particularly the more liberal Protestant groups—turned to psychoanalysis as a means of improving the counseling which always had been part of their work. "Pastoral coun-seling" became part of the seminary curriculum in many in-stances. Periodicals such as *Pastoral Psychology* sought to broaden older ministers' psychological knowledge and offered counselors help in handling their parishioners' problems. In work with young people, for example, church counseling tried to apply psychological concepts of human development and to help adolescents cope with their difficulties in growing up. This the churches sought to do in consonance with religious doctrine, not always an easy task—for in considerable measure the churches held to standards (of sexual morality particularly) which were sufficiently restrictive to inspire a sense of guilt in young people.

Presently some effort is being made, too, to apply analytic insights to religious behavior. Instead of being indignant that certain religious doctrines should be linked with obsessional reaction-formations, some clergymen are trying to use psychoanalysis to purge the religious life of neurosis. Clergymen, secular and monastic, have long been familiar with the scrupulousness that moves some people to carry their proper feeling of unworthiness before the Lord beyond reason until it becomes a source of torment. Such cases can properly be dealt with by psychoanalysis alone, many clerically oriented therapists contend, since an obsessional neurosis is in operation, not merely an unusually refined tenderness of conscience.

Some defenders of faith insist that Freud was really one of themselves. Because he endured pain through long years without flinching, because he never compromised his scientific beliefs but continued his work despite opposition, because he bore himself bravely before his Nazi conquerors, and because he regarded ethical behavior as socially imperative, Freud has been called a truly religious person, whatever his own disclaimers. (Those are asserted to be merely an instance of the psychoanalytically defined mechanism of denial.[16])

Gregory Zilboorg, for instance, maintains that not only was Freud a believer without knowing it, but a Catholic believer at that—as is shown by the importance of the date of Easter in his dreams. Freud's atheism, according to Zilboorg, was a mere reaction to betrayed affection for a pious nurse. She had taken him to church with her when he was young, had taught him the essentials of Catholic belief, and had made an indelible impression upon his affection and his mind.[17] She was discharged for theft and he never saw her again. Because this loved figure did not return to him—and because of the guilt Freud had felt at this time for wishing his younger

[16] Zilboorg, *Freud and Religion*, p. 62.
[17] Zilboorg, *Psychoanalysis and Religion*, pp. 239–41.

brother dead, he had repudiated God and faith.[18] But, Zilboorg concludes, his hostility to religion was no less a neurotic
phenomenon than he asserted religion itself to be.

By 1962, the rapprochement between analyst and clergyman
had progressed to such a degree that one contributor to the
Atlantic Monthly's 1962 symposium on psychiatry in American life found it appropriate to remind both lion and lamb
that there were basic points of difference between religion
and psychoanalysis and that these might be summed up thus:
the analyst wants man to be independent, recognizing no
master but reality; the priest wants man to be dependent on
God and the church. To give Freud the final word: "If one
can find a new argument against the truth of religion by
applying the psychoanalytic method, so much the worse for
religion, but the defenders of religion will with equal right
avail themselves of psychoanalysis in order to appreciate to
the full the affective significance of religious doctrine."

[18] *Future of an Illusion,* pp. 65–66.

7 · Reflections on Post-Analytic America

7 · Reflections on Post-Analytic America

We have described how Freudian theory came to the United States and how, after years of opposition, it has come to affect and suffuse many aspects of American life. Our primary interest has been the cultural setting in which psychoanalysis came of age in America. For thus we can most clearly relate the development of psychoanalysis to certain aspects of the contemporary situation and to some of the special problems the individual in midcentury America confronts as he seeks to maintain his psychological integrity in an organizational type of mass society.

Psychoanalysis owes its success in the United States to coincidental changes in the American cultural setting on the one hand and to the modifications which have been made in the practice and theory of psychotherapy on the other. Without the revisions which the neo- and post-Freudians have brought to psychoanalysis, one may doubt whether it would have been as attractive to middle-class Americans. Without the continuing revolt which engaged American intellectuals after 1900, they would have been less susceptible to Freudian influence. The American's readiness to welcome novelty is largely responsible for the incorporation of analysis as a significant element in our culture. European observers see all philosophies, and even religious faith itself, as but shallowly rooted among Americans from whom the constant social flux

[163]

which they experience does indeed elicit a certain superficiality of response. But that superficiality has, as its other side, a flexibility which makes it possible for new ideas like Freud's to win widespread acceptance. Flexibility may mean open-mindedness, particularly awareness that existing value systems are insufficient for existing needs and a willingness to seek both support for values, and values themselves, in increased self-understanding.

But this alone is too simplistic a view, one that does not take sufficient account of the inherent liberating character of Freudian theory. Thomas Mann declared that one day Freud would be honored not only as an intellectual pioneer but as the pathfinder to a humanism of the future, one ". . . standing in a different relation to the powers of the lower world, the unconscious, the id; a relation bolder, freer, blither, productive of a riper art than any possible in our neurotic, fear-ridden, hate-ridden world."[1]

Those especially who complain that too much of contemporary American psychotherapy concerns itself merely with making individuals tolerate their existence may consider it unrealistic to suggest that psychoanalysis can free a sufficient number of people to change man's relation to himself and his world. But would it not have seemed equally unrealistic to think in the early decades of the twentieth century that Freud's long struggle to win recognition for psychoanalysis would achieve the kind of victory represented by the current position of psychoanalysis in the United States?

In this country, some forms of psychoanalysis have become almost a way of life. However superficial the understanding of psychoanalytic concepts may be, however much Freudian insights may be distorted or diluted, those insights have affected every aspect of American thinking and much of our behavior as well. Few academic disciplines have escaped the influence of Freud's ideas. The anthropologist studies the

[1] Thomas Mann, "Freud and the Future," in *Freud, Goethe and Wagner* (New York: Knopf, 1937).

primitive family less in terms of the formal organization of relationships (who are forbidden as mates, for example, and such relationships on the rearing of children. The sociologist who are preferred or prescribed) than in terms of the effect of has been provoked to examine the interplay between an unusually mobile society and a rather labile individual. The political scientist has had to become aware of the sexual aspect of men's attraction to political leaders and of their willingness to continue cooperation in political parties. The economist may take account of Freudian formulations when he attempts to understand men's motives for the accumulation of capital. The psychologist tries to ascertain, to observe, and sometimes to measure men's attitudes and their behavior. Even the historian has learned to use a number of psychoanalytic concepts, not merely as tools for understanding the motivation of the individuals and the groups whose behavior he describes but, more importantly perhaps, as a means of improving his own approach to his material by being made far more delicately aware of his own biases. Finally, children are differently reared in the American home, somewhat differently taught at school, and often differently dealt with, when they clash with public authority. Many an American child has been spared needless unhappiness because conscientious mothers have learned something about the consequences of premature toilet training in which they themselves have an irrational emotional stake. Many a present-day American classroom is governed by a teacher who has learned at least some facts about children's emotional development and its relation to their ability to learn. Current handling of the problems of young people in trouble may be inadequate, but awareness of that inadequacy is keener, and understanding of what needs to be done is more realistic because psychoanalytic concepts have filtered down through the society. It is this widespread and pervasive character of Freudian influence in these and other areas that makes it reasonable to speak of "post-analytic America."

American Rebelliousness and the Freudian Revolt

Freud's Worcester visit and his lectures at Clark University symbolized more than the initiation of a new American profession or even the introduction and development of a more scientific psychotherapy. Freud brought his theories to an America which was restive, uneasy under old restrictive conventions, although paradoxically ready to accept and impose such new ones as Prohibition. It was to this America that Freud brought his ideas about how men might relate to themselves.

The United States has been described as the place where Victorian morality found its most ludicrous expression. The eighteenth century was forthright: John Adams wrote, "Man's first want is his dinner and his second his girl." The early nineteenth century was prudish: by the 1830's, "legs" became "limbs," and a British visitor, the forgotten but then popular novelist Captain Frederick Marryat, described an American parlor where ruffled pantalettes made the legs of a piano modest.

Yet in certain respects, American society imposed fewer restrictions upon sexuality than European society. We have mentioned the relative liberality of American divorce laws before the Civil War. It is less generally known that America was then somewhat liberal in regard to the spread of contraceptive information. Young John Stuart Mill, later to be famous as an economist and social philosopher, was taken into custody, brought before a London magistrate, lectured, and discharged only on account of his "respectable" connections—because he had tried to distribute an American pamphlet on birth control.

American women had long been equally famed for their chastity and for the freedom of their manners. The renowned womanizer, the Duc de Lauzun, recorded no conquests in those pages of his memoirs which describe his years serving in the French army that came to Washington's aid in 1778. But Lauzun was as much struck by the liberty which American young girls enjoyed as by their severe virtue. And for many decades thereafter, Europeans continued to marvel at the way in which American girls and boys danced and picnicked, drove and went to the theater, all unchaperoned— and all without apparent increase in the proportion of illegitimate births.

By 1900, coeducation had become quite common, especially in the state universities of the Middle and Far West. Women generally controlled their own property even after marriage. They were enjoying the suffrage in a few states and demanding it in many others. And although feminism did in this period carry certain overtones of hostility to men, it may also have concealed an expression of the middle-class American woman's longing for greater sexual freedom.[2]

One might more accurately call the America which Freud visited more prudish, not more sexually repressive than the Europe of his day. That visible prudery might be attributed to two factors: the social dominance of the middle class and the publicly recognized influence of the middle-class woman; and the influence of the middle-class woman was formidable, not only because the class to which she belonged dominated the society but also because aesthetic culture had all but formally been made her ward. She staffed the schools and often, as parent, concerned herself with their operation, with what and how they taught. She might even hold administrative posts, which gave her further control over the content of education and over methods of teaching. She had time and money to spend on books and magazines; she operated the libraries; she attended the lectures; her tastes and diffidences ruled the market and exercised a censorship far more effec-

[2] Although the first phase of feminism uses a vocabulary strongly laced with phrases like a "single standard of morals," meaning that young men should be required to come to marriage as unsullied as their presumably virgin brides, one may regard that as hostility to male dictation of the *mores* rather than to hostility to men or to sex *per se*.

tive than any imposed by law. Insofar as she was prudish, the society would be prudish; insofar as her prudery relaxed, the society's attitude would be altered.

Although the middle-class woman was thus influential, she was also far from certain of herself; she felt her tastes in need of guidance. She was eager to learn, or at any event to imitate those who called themselves her cultural betters. To a certain degree, she was malleable, and the more because of her own changing economic and educational situation. As parent and teacher, as wife, mother, and female, she was accessible to Freudian influence.

But the middle-class woman was not the only insecure, yet influential segment of American society. Intellectuals too were experiencing continuous pressures. One effect of the country's participation in the First World War was to increase insecurity, even while it tended to make the *mores* less restrictive, at least among intellectuals and the more prosperous urban middle class. The war which inflicted a catastrophic blow on Europe fostered both economic expansion and a kind of social liberation in the United States. The decades before the war had seen a great ploughing up of certainties, legal, philosophical, political, even economic. American intellectuals' attention veered away from politics after 1920, but they became still more restless socially, and that restlessness opened the way for further penetration of Freudian theory. Psychoanalysis, in its turn, both contributed to the disintegration of certainties and seemed to hold out some promise of replacing what had been lost, not by helping men create new and more effective restraints but by freeing an increasing number of persons from the need to depend on external restrictions.

Replacing the support given by old certainties (though not the certainties themselves) seemed the more necessary because the society was mobile; the impact of technological change upon it was (and continues to be) unblunted. The influence of what may be termed its "official interpreters" was unstable and of unlimited authority. The Catholic clergy, who did have real power to direct their people's thinking, ministered, by and large, to a lower-class group; American intellectual leaders were not much affected by them. The Protestant clergy enjoyed formal respect, but the intellectual leaders of the day did not treat them as authoritative guides. Philosophers, scholars, and scientists were not seen as figures of authority by the public, however.[3] Businessmen were widely venerated for the money they had made, to be sure, but neither they nor their ghost writers had more than platitudes to offer to people who, often without even recognizing their need, felt a desire for an understanding of, and some emotional anchorage in, a kaleidoscopic world.

Again the way was open for psychoanalysis to affect the thinking of the relatively sophisticated person who was alert to other needs and other possibilities in existence than the moneymaking which has brought, and continues to bring, meaning into so many American lives. But even the less sophisticated American was, in some measure, ready for at least a kind of self-examination. Psychoanalysis, with its direction of attention to the meaning of even trivial behavior, reinforces self-awareness and self-exploration. Hence it seemed in accord with what had long been recognized as an American trait, willingness to explore and describe their own and their society's character; psychoanalysis was especially congenial to a number of persons who were already investigating American life on their own.

Therapy in a Changing America

As has been said earlier, therapists who continue to practice classical psychoanalysis sometimes deny that their revisionist

[3] It may seem contradictory to deny social authority to intellectuals when discussing the spread of Freudian thought, in which intellectuals necessarily had to act as interpreters. But American culture's very lack of regard for any kind of thinking unrelated to immediate practical ends makes Americans peculiarly non-resistant to such thoughts when it is persuasively presented, when it does not directly challenge the existing structure of economic and political power, and when, in addition, it is spiced with what was once regarded as titillating reference to sex.

colleagues are doing analysis at all, so radical do their modifications of theory and of technique appear, at least at first
glance. Although many classicists recognize the significance
of the neo-Freudian argument that analysis must accommodate
to the needs of a changing patient (and their own emphasis
on ego psychology constitutes such a recognition), they insist, and with some justice, that the neo-Freudians still have
not established an agreed theoretical basis for their procedures;
hence, however useful revisionist therapy may be in certain
situations, it is not, the classicists contend, psychoanalysis.

The innovators, for their part, admit that the classicists' ob-
jection may be well taken, but they continue to assert the need
for change. It may seem unnecessary even to mention the
difference between the cultural setting in which Freud developed psychoanalysis—the Vienna of the Austro-Hungarian
Empire and the defeated Austrian Republic—and the metropolitan areas in which psychoanalysis flourishes in the United
States. Yet workers in the behavioral sciences must discuss
the obvious because the implications of the obvious so often
escape our attention. Freud's own patients generally came
from the upper bourgeoisie and he thought analytic treatment
of lower-class patients would be quite difficult. Prosperous
though the American patient may be, he often belongs to
what Freud's Vienna would have regarded as a lower class.
Rarely is the American who comes to therapy even a relatively leisured person; he must earn his living. Since he faces
the need to find and hold a suitable job and balance a budget,
he has far more need to discuss immediately personal socio-
economic problems (especially as those relate to his relationships with superiors and co-workers) than did the typical
patient in Freud's practice. Methods which served Freud in
prewar Vienna, methods which were adequate for Brill and
his followers in interwar New York, are not suited to the
needs of the midcentury American patient. Today's therapist
encounters a psychologically sophisticated person who has
developed new patterns of resistance and whose neuroses mani-

fest themselves in symptoms markedly different from those common in earlier generations. Hence it is reasonable for the therapist to alter not only his clinical methods but also his concept of the purpose of analytic therapy.

The diffusion of psychoanalytic insights and of the jargon of analysis has made people more willing to enter treatment, but it has also given birth to new varieties of resistance: today's patient often uses his information as a means of defending himself against the kind of knowledge, and more important, against the kind of emotional response, which will help him change his neurotic attitudes and behavior. Further, new applications of psychotherapy and the rising demand for it have brought into the field persons of very different background and training. Social workers and ministers, for example, may act as psychological counselors with no thorough instruction; sometimes they attempt group therapy with equally insufficient preparation. Since the number of those who attempt to practice some kind of psychotherapy has increased far beyond the facilities for teaching them, it is rather more than less likely that the psychoanalytic content of such therapy will be both diluted and distorted. Occasionally patients come into treatment with more conventionally trained therapists after spending time with such counselors, and the therapist is then confronted with further problems of resistance, for such patients often have attitudes and expectations that may impose barriers to effective work in therapy.

In addition to encountering patterns of resistance very different from those common in the early decades of psychoanalysis, today's analyst encounters patients with new kinds of emotional disorder. He sees few hysterics; he sees many borderline schizophrenics; he sees more people still who present no very definite pattern of symptoms, but who instead present difficulties involving an inability to meet the demands of contemporary life. This incapacity can often be traced to a failure of, or disturbance in, the patient's sense of identity. He does not know who or even what he is. Therefore, he cannot know what, if anything, he is for; he lacks purpose; he cannot envision a goal which is worth the effort needed to reach it.

Patients of this sort are inclined to seek direction. Often they seem so unable to relate to other people and so unfamiliar with their own emotions that the therapist must interpret not their dreams but their social relations; he must even describe their emotions to them. The psychoanalyst of the old stereotype—the wise, kindly, yet wholly uninvolved person—cannot meet the needs of such patients. Being well versed in the basic principles of psychoanalytic practice and theory is no longer sufficient preparation for therapy. In contemporary America, the analyst who limits himself to the classical view of his profession cannot function as effectively as the analyst who understands current cultural patterns and is alert to the intricate interplay between individual and society, between the patient's need to live in society as it is (and so recognize reality) and awareness that our present organizational society often tends to starve people emotionally, to deprive them of the kinds of stability that make growth possible. The analyst is not called upon to change that world, of course, nor is his function as a therapist to urge the patient to act on that level. But the contemporary analyst cannot afford to be isolated from the world; insight into the universal, the instinctual, aspects of the patient's life history is not enough. The analyst must be conversant with the peculiar anxieties that beset many people in this culture. Only this wider outlook will enable him to show patients how they, in the world they inhabit, can free themselves sufficiently to control their lives, choose their goals, and develop their potentialities. The existential analyst who places himself *in the world* and knows, in terms of his own existence, the trials and tribulations of his patients is far better equipped to help than the classicist. Understanding of and empathetic insight into the existential despair, loneliness, and alienation, which the analyst sees as characteristic of so many people's experience, will serve him in the treatment of his patients.

A broader view of psychoanalysis than the strictly clinical does not constitute too drastic a departure from Freud's own approach. He did not even agree that restricting the practice of psychoanalysis to physicians would prevent its exploitation by charlatans. Indeed, he wrote: "I make bold to assert that doctors furnish the largest contingent of quacks in analysis— and not only in European countries."[4] And the author of *Totem and Taboo* scarcely would have the psychoanalyst restrict his view to the patient on his couch. Freud would, in all likelihood, agree that the present influence of psychotherapy and of his own work in the United States is not to be explained merely by the American intellectual's love of novelty and his continued need for support of his rebelliousness. The impact of the Second World War is to be taken into account and the increasing tempo of technological change thereafter.

The war, which ended the Great Depression, gave numbers of people money to buy goods. It stimulated the growth of computer-governed kinds of mechanization which have yet to make themselves fully felt. The stalemated power struggle which followed the Second World War has operated to sustain purchasing power by requiring high levels of governmental spending, to increase the rate of technological change, at least in certain areas of industry, and to heighten psychological irritations growing out of an awareness that the "return-to-normalcy" philosophy of the 1920's will not work in the 1960's, no matter how many Americans vote for it.

Moreover, in spite of a high level of prosperity, social problems continue to accumulate, and these (although rather successfully avoided for a time) as irritants intensifying anxieties. Consider, for example, contemporary aspects of urbanization. Fewer than a sixth of the people of the United States now earn their living in agriculture, but the traditional city is tending to disappear along with the old-fashioned family farm. Instead of the relatively stable, though untidy, growth of the

[4] Sigmund Freud, *The Question of Lay Analysis* (New York: Norton, 1950), pp. 91–92.

past, when blight and renewal spread and receded within a rather confined area, we have "urban sprawl." Men flee the crowding, noise, and dirt of the central city, and in their flight they carry all three into what was the countryside.

It is in these metropolitan areas—one can call them neither country nor city—where growth has so far outrun the capacity of existing political organization to deal with the problems of growth that we note the most obvious effects on the personality. In the central city, according to a recent study of mental health in mid-Manhattan,[5] persons of every religious denomination and of every income level reveal problems which show that about 20 per cent of the persons questioned have emotional problems serious enough to require treatment, yet only a small proportion of them are receiving any kind of therapy. But, emotional distress is to be found even in well-to-do suburbia. It may seem surprising that anxiety should be so severe among people whose material needs are so fully met and whose family life is so intensely cultivated, but the records of alcoholism, divorce, juvenile delinquency, emotional breakdown, and the prevalence of apathy cannot be ignored.

The problems of the new urbanization are in large part an outgrowth of the physical and social mobility which makes "settling down" so difficult. People who have cars can live far from their jobs, but travel takes time and a long daily trip to work hampers the growth of diversified communities; the suburbs are often inhabited by women and children; the men come home for leisure. Professionals and businessmen, too, must go where jobs and their employers require; the middle class is no longer a stable presence in a community. Americans have always been mobile, but the mobility of our time has made uprooting into a kind of pattern. It has not yet jelled into a style of life, although that style may be emerging. The standardized environment of highway, shopping center, and housing development which seems so dreary to outsiders and

[5] Leo Snole, *et al, Mental Health in the Metropolis* (New York: McGraw-Hill, 1962).

which is becoming so characteristically the American scene may correspond to a need to make mobility less visible. The adaptable person, who presents no uncomfortable edges of opinion, of sharply individual taste, of attachment to places or persons, may perhaps foreshadow the future American. As the ancient Greeks extolled the man who was beautiful and good, as the nineteenth-century English revered the "gentleman," so the twentieth-century American emulates the man who, like a well-engineered mobile unit, "fits in anywhere you put him."[6]

Yet many men want, or sincerely believe they ought to want, to be unique individuals. Such people feel they have lost command: in varying measure, they are aware of the pressure of outside forces that affect not only the conditions of their lives but even their purpose for living. Such pressure contravenes the desire for self-direction; the ensuing awareness of being helpless generates anxiety. And anxious Americans inhabit both the urban jungle and the pleasant spaces of the suburbs.

As has been noted, some American receptivity to psychoanalysis may be attributable to modifications of Freudian theory. More important is the continuing need for help. In earlier periods, persons with emotional problems could use friends or relatives as confidants. Now people find it difficult to express feelings of uncertainty or distress not only because of their own pride but because their anxiety increases the anxiety already present in those to whom it is communicated.

The very notion of friendship and confidence has altered. Once, friendship developed slowly until friends felt themselves to be emotional counterparts. Currently, in the United States the distinction between friend and acquaintance tends to blur. More people are called *friends*, but often they are

[6] See Hendrik M. Ruitenbeek, ed., *The Dilemma of an Organizational Society* (New York: E. P. Dutton, 1963); see also, David Riesman, *The Lonely Crowd* (New Haven: Yale University Press, 1950); William H. Whyte, Jr., *The Organization Man* (New York: Doubleday Anchor, 1956); Ruitenbeek, *The Individual and the Crowd* (New York: New American Library, 1965).

known as part of a group rather than felt to be involved with oneself alone. And, of course, relatives—at least among the sophisticated—are regarded as the source of emotional problems rather than resources for dealing with those problems. It seems safer to unburden oneself to a psychotherapist, not only because he is an expert and trained to help but because, being a paid professional, one need not become involved, as is necessarily the case when one talks to a person one knows and has regard for. Many people seem to act as if the only person they could trust to listen was somebody hired for the job. Such deepseated loneliness and isolation confronts the psychotherapist with a problem mentioned earlier: how shall man be reconciled to the conditions of his existence?

The Future of Analytic Therapy

As we have said, traditional philosophy and traditional religion have proved inadequate to man's needs in the crisis-ridden world which Spengler forecast so accurately in his *Decline of the West*. This statement does not imply that people no longer turn to the traditional resources, for the world, in our time, changes faster than men adopt new methods for dealing with it. But as individuals find customary sources of support inadequate when they do try to use them, psycho-analysis tends to become an increasingly important factor in the culture.[7]

The psychotherapist cannot but realize that he now treats people who must function within a society affected, almost created, by crisis and generating pressures which grow more intense as the crisis is felt more generally—though not always consciously. Many people seem less and less able to accept their lives or to find real meaning in them. On the other hand, a sizable number of persons seem entirely ready to accept

[7] Thomas Szasz, "Psychiatry as a Social Institution," in *Psychiatry and Responsibility*, Helmut Schoeck and James W. Wiggins, eds. (New York: D. Van Nostrand Co., Inc., 1962), p. 9.

lives without meaning. These people, too, may seek psycho-therapy, but less as a means of achieving growth than as a method for fashioning a "good adjustment"—a phrase sug-gesting the mechanical. (Surprisingly few people seem at all reluctant to talk of themselves in terms of a mechanism with a bearing in need of grease, although not long ago only the eccentric or the emotionally disturbed person was said to have a "screw loose.")

Acceptance of things as they are colors much professional thinking in the social disciplines in the United States. Gen-eralizations are out of favor because they might be developed into an "ideology," and ideology has become a term of abuse along with "idealism." Conservatism is the current fashion. Aspiration is suspect, particularly aspiration toward improv-ing social conditions, and the suspicion with which aspiration is regarded is often bolstered by notions and phrases derived from Freudian thought. Thus, the expression of altruistic impulses is often interpreted as evidence of hidden real hos-tility. Concern for the public welfare is sometimes called eva-sion of one's own problems, and the desire to move toward personal goodness is frequently treated as a matter fit only for private shame and public ridicule. Kenneth Keniston even suggests that men now tend to repress what an earlier time would have called *our higher selves*: the contemporary id holds not the sexual but the political libido.[8]

With all ideologies suspect, psychoanalysis more and more is taken as a source of insights for helping people define their goals, their values, and their relationships to other people. Psychoanalysis in the United States has matured in a context of what the existentialist would describe as a culture-in-crisis and an individual-in-crisis. Psychoanalysis has changed as a result, and it will continue to change as the country changes. No problem in the social sciences, which reflect the state of

[8] Kenneth Keniston, "Alienation and the Decline of Utopia," *American Scholar*, XXIX, Spring, 1960; also in Hendrik M. Ruitenbeek, ed., *Varieties of Modern Social Theory* (New York: E. P. Dutton & Co., Inc., 1963).

the culture even as they examine it, can be approached without taking into account material drawn from psychoanalysis. This trend will continue during the coming decades, for psychoanalysis is far from having reached the limits of its applicability. The individual in our society will continue to have problems and he will continue to seek resolution of those problems in psychoanalysis since traditional religious faiths, conventional philosophies, inherited political ideologies no longer provide him with adequate bases for emotional stability.

He will have problems not only because he experiences what all men must experience, the tensions of growth and adaptation to culture, but also because he experiences those immemorial tensions as he grows up and lives in a highly organized economy constantly being changed because of technological developments. He is very likely to suffer from anxiety generated by swift and often unpredictable transformations. For he seems unable either to do without what technology and the organizational society can provide or to make that society livable. In proportion to his education, to his income, and to his psychological sophistication, he will seek psychoanalytic help.

And psychotherapists will try to provide that help. By its very nature, psychoanalysis deals with the individual. Fromm and Horney have stressed the role of society in the interaction between society and the individual, but they have proceeded from basic analytic principles. And these principles require that the analyst, when working in the context of therapy, avoid involvement with any conventional set of value judgments. Psychoanalysis cannot commit itself to a social or philosophic program. In the limited context of therapy itself, psychoanalysis is a modest procedure; it does not venture on prognosis; the therapist usually refuses to predict the outcome of treatment. The patient shows he has understood what psychoanalysis is when he stops asking his analyst to tell him when he will "get well" and what he will be like when he does.

Psychoanalysis will continue to help some persons. It will continue to contribute insights which other people may use to learn to know themselves better, whether they go into therapy or not. Hopefully, one outcome of this increased knowledge will be a greater number of fulfilled lives or, at least, a smaller number of thwarted existences.

The Dimension of Values

Throughout this discussion, there has been at least an implicit concern with the relationship between psychoanalysis and the problem of values. The lessened influence of accepted social imperatives gave psychoanalysis its first opportunity to affect the American intellectual who had lost his earlier confidence in philosophical and religious sources of guidance. Further depletion of traditional sources of psychological security—the family, the church, and the stable face-to-face community—caused more and more Americans to suffer from emotional disturbance and to seek analytic treatment. The problems they brought to therapy influenced analysts like Burrow, Fromm, and Horney to consider more carefully the interrelationship between socially generated pressure and emotional distress. Patients in surprising numbers appeared to be asking that psychoanalysis give them something different from what patients sought before 1914 or even during the 1920's and early 1930's. American patients were, at midcentury, evidently suffering less from specific symptoms than from inability to find genuine satisfaction in their lives. Freud had defined the adult and healthy person as one who was able to love and to work. Many patients seemed more than merely sexually impotent or emotionally incapable of love; they did not appear to know what adult love meant. And often, amid the complexities of earning a living in a large organization—business, government, or academic—their work appeared to be activity almost divorced from intrinsic meaning.

Patients whose lives left them thus empty sought something beyond relief of their neurotic symptoms. Whether they used the phrase or not, they wanted therapy to help them find goals in life. They transformed the psychoanalyst into the "wise man" of tradition. Consequently, despite an essential modesty of aspiration, psychoanalysis is beginning to shape or at least to color men's values, particularly as those are involved in the relationship between the individual and his society.

In *Civilization and Its Discontents,* Freud presents his definitive statement of what psychoanalysis regards as the relationship between the needs of man as an individual and as a member of society. Freud identifies civilization with repression of instinctual drives. The murder of the "primal father" is, he declares, a "psychical" reality. In his words:

It is not really a decisive matter whether one has killed one's father or abstained from the deed; one must feel guilty in either case, for guilt is the expression of the conflict of ambivalence, the eternal struggle between Eros and the destructive or death instinct. This conflict is engendered as soon as man is confronted with the task of living with his fellows; as long as he knows no other form of life in common but that of the family, it must express itself in the Oedipus complex, cause the development of conscience, and create the first feelings of guilt. When mankind tries to institute wider forms of communal life, the same conflict continues to arise—in forms derived from the past—and intensified so that a further reinforcement of the sense of guilt results. Since culture obeys an inner erotic impulse which bids it bind mankind into a closely knit mass, it can achieve this aim only by means of its vigilance in fomenting an ever-increasing sense of guilt.[9]

If Freud is taken strictly, there appears to be little hope for civilized man: he must suffer as an individual from suppression of his instinctual needs. Or, as individual or group, he must suffer the consequences when those suppressed instinctual drives burst forth to express themselves in social conflict.

The Nazis' repudiation of civilization, the ever-accelerating transformation of warfare into an exercise in mass slaughter, the apparent worldwide repudiation of existing civilization

[9] Freud, *Civilization and Its Discontents* (New York: Norton, 1964, reissue).

by so many young people—all seem to show that Freud was right. Some of his successors agree that men do indeed experience conflict between their instinctual needs and the demands of their society, but this conflict is the price man pays for living in human culture, and the price, they maintain, is worth paying. Neo-Freudians—Karen Horney, Harry Stack Sullivan, and Erich Fromm among them—see the issue differently. Human culture, they argue, is the means by which man realizes his nature rather than a burden imposed upon that nature by an evolutionary process.[10]

Current discussions of the relationship between psychoanalysis and society have focused on the validity of Freud's view of man and on whether men, being of such character, can change their social behavior. Post- and neo-Freudians usually hold that treatment of the neurotic patient cannot proceed successfully unless the therapist is aware of the interrelationship between the individual personality and the culture in which it develops. Erikson finds that an "anal" personality has been formed as the result of the rise of Protestantism and capitalism. Fromm, similarly, declares that much of our psychological misery is produced by capitalist society. For this society, he contends, has not provided goals people feel to be meaningful; nor has it helped the individual achieve a sufficient sense of identity and self-esteem. Some social scientists—David Riesman and Allen Wheelis, for instance—have been sufficiently influenced by neo-Freudian theory to describe the contemporary American as an alienated person.

It is surprising to see these opinions winning such large audiences in a country so completely committed to capitalism, but no more surprising really than the success of psychoanalysis in the same country. Both these phenomena, it seems likely, have occurred because of the instability of existence in America and because, for Americans, the separation between opinion and political action is so evident and so easy.

[10] Hans Meyerhoff, "Freud and the Ambiguity of Culture," *Partisan Review*, No. 1, Winter, 1957.

Although it is a century since the United States has known
the movement of armies in battle across its soil, the "ordinary"
life of an American subjects him to a disorganizing flux of
experience to a far greater degree than is common in Europe.
Of course, the need to live in flux has always been part of the
American's social experience; but the process has accelerated
since the First World War.

In the nineteenth century, people could apprehend their
existence in terms of their immediate surroundings and the
relationships occurring within them. That, and that alone, constituted their world. What happened outside the orbit of that
limited experience did not much affect their interpretation of
their existence. Life on that level required no large frame
of reference. What framework did seem necessary to the
average man was supplied by a set of standards, social and
religious, which most people thought of as existing independently outside themselves, like the sun, and which were,
like the sunlight, to be accepted and absorbed without questioning. Birth, illness, marriage, death, failure, success, all were
accepted as occurrences, not as problems. When personal
difficulties did arise, people handled them in silence (coping
or suffering as their temperament and capacity permitted)
or by talking to their intimates. Sometimes they might take
such problems to a clergyman or, more rarely, to a doctor
who was felt to be a friend.

In our day, the psychotherapist, listening to similar problems, is aware that they are often associated with a weakening
of both ego and superego, a weakening which makes it needful
for him to look at society (whose commands are incorporated
into the superego and to which the ego must adapt) if he is
really to understand his patient. Allen Wheelis and David
Riesman are but two of the social scientists who seek to show
how individual character is being altered by the changing
outside world. Wheelis sees the American as a man in search
of an identity. He must engage in this search because the conditions of life in his society prevent his following the traditional path toward discovering and establishing identity. Until

rather recently, that discovery could be made without taking thought; one absorbed patterns of behavior and feeling from the environment and made those patterns one's own through the process of internalization. Those internalized standards then provided reasonably adequate guidance for one's life.[11] Now, however, the environment appears to be incapable of providing the necessary standards. Many values once taken for granted have become irrelevant in the twentieth century. Although people continue to give them lip service, they feel— buffeted as they are by the currents of technological change —that the eternal verities to which they pledge such intense verbal allegiance actually do not exist.

Awareness of change as the norm of life has created the kind of social character which will accept psychoanalysis as a method for dealing with neurotic suffering. In the early and middle nineteenth century, when ego and superego could develop within a context of values that most people regarded as relevant, worthy, and stable, psychoanalysis would probably have been rejected as a gross intrusion upon the patient's privacy.

Like other human beings, however, the American requires some source of guidance. He finds that in his peer group, Riesman says. The process begins in childhood, is grotesquely evident in youth, and continues through life, producing what Riesman calls the "other-directed" personality. Rather than incorporating social "rules" and then treating them as if they were wholly his own—as the "inner-directed" personality did and continues to do—the other-directed person strives to catch the clue to what "the others" are thinking and then to behave accordingly. While all else is changing, this striving to adapt to the others is the "constant." The goals, the actual content of behavior and opinion may shift,[12] but attention to what the "others" are doing is unvarying. But "the others"

[11] Allen Wheelis, *The Quest for Identity* (New York: Norton, 1958), p. 164.
[12] David Riesman, *The Lonely Crowd* (New Haven: Yale University Press, 1950), p. 22.

also respond to external clues. Some of these clues come from the mass media and, since profit is the principal objective of those media, the clues generally signal "go buy something." Such signals support behavior which sustains the economy, but they do not inspire the individual with a sense of personal worth apart from the goods he can buy and show off. Further, because the individual knows that he is trying to learn what his peers are doing (since in one way or another he is aware that he is following) he feels that he has no real desires of his own.

Dependence on one's contemporaries of the kind Riesman describes does not build either a strong superego or a strong ego. The other-directed man feels obliged to act as his peers do, but that obligation is not embedded in the unconscious as the traditionally acquired superego is. The commands of other-direction shift, particularly because they are subject to the kind of manipulation which large-circulation magazines, television, and radio make possible. The other-directed person plays his social roles. He develops the structured patterns of behavior he is expected to show, but he feels neither role nor behavior to be genuinely and fully his own. In consequence, he feels himself adrift, without governing purpose; he experiences what the sociologist calls *anomie*. Alienation and anxiety accompany this experience. The ego, too, seems to lack force. The other-directed person who comes to psychotherapy often talks as if he had not only lost his bearings, but as if he had never had any bearings, had never grasped any effective and dependable guidelines for his life.

In this situation, where the individual experiences unremitting pressures from without and cannot discover within himself resources strong enough to help him withstand those pressures, he is apt to seek in psychotherapy a kind of help which classical analysis never envisaged and which even the contemporary neo-Freudian therapist may not be at all equipped to give. (Here one cannot but help remember James Putnam and his insistence that psychoanalysis needed to be set into a general philosophical framework if it was to realize its full potential.) The demand will be made, however, and today's therapist may find himself all but forced to fulfil this part of his patients' needs. It would be well that he act in awareness that he is imparting values; it would be well, too, that he examine the values he, however unwillingly, imparts.

Conclusion

We have surveyed the arrival and reception of Freudian theory in the United States. We have seen how it was denounced, sometimes even without real examination, then examined critically, then gradually accepted, popularized, and diluted. We have also seen how, since 1909, psychoanalysis has affected every aspect of American intellectual life and has colored many contemporary American attitudes.

The impact of Freud on the United States may be best understood in terms of its character as a society. The United States was dynamic; many sources of psychological stability were decreasingly effective in providing emotional security for the individuals who had to live amid such rapid change. In accepting psychoanalysis in ways far different from Europeans, Americans showed their ability to grasp and adapt to their own needs a new interpretation of human behavior and the development of human character. Such awareness and appreciation is an instance of foresight not common in the history of civilizations.

Freud was surprised to find the United States so ready to give psychoanalysis a hearing and to accept it, but we may be less surprised, for we have seen how that acceptance has paralleled the changes in American society since 1910. Always mobile, Americans have become more mobile still. Always somewhat insecure, intellectually and psychologically—reflecting, perhaps, a colonial past—Americans, more than Europeans, have been ready to examine their society and themselves and to accept insight, wherever it could be found.

Since 1929, all of the Western world has experienced depression, war, and the constrictions imposed by life in an organizational society. Other countries have suffered more from war and conquest. Few have endured the pressures of organizational society so long and with so sharp, so direct an impact. Many sensitive Americans, therefore, feel peculiarly lost in their own culture. The less sensitive may not be so actually aware of suffering, but their disquiet can be inferred from the "emotional casualty lists": the statistics for mental illness, alcoholism, drug addiction, delinquency, divorce, and suicide. In the 1950's, especially, many Americans found that their society gave them only an unreliable kind of emotional support, for guidance from the peer group, which had tended to replace so many of the traditional guides, provided but a wavering psychological staff. Since strength could not be reliably obtained from outside, it had to be sought within. But too often, the person who looked within seemed to find nothing there. He experienced loneliness and isolation with bitter immediacy. Some people married and begot large families and cultivated a "togetherness" which they hoped would encapsulate them and theirs from the pain and risks of "living in the world." Others turned to psychoanalysis in search of support, and even in search of identity—for the self which the conditions of life in America did so little to foster.

Index